Brian Haynes

SHIFT

What it takes to *finally* reach families today

Incredible things will happen™
LOVELAND, COLORADO
group.com

Group resources actually work!

This Group resource incorporates our R.E.A.L. approach to ministry. It reinforces a growing friendship with Jesus, encourages long-term learning, and results in life transformation, because it's

Relational
Learner-to-learner interaction enhances learning and builds Christian friendships.

Experiential
What learners experience through discussion and action sticks with them up to 9 times longer than what they simply hear or read.

Applicable
The aim of Christian education is to equip learners to be both hearers and doers of God's Word.

Learner-based
Learners understand and retain more when the learning process takes into consideration how they learn best.

Shift
What It Takes to *Finally* Reach Families Today
Copyright © 2009 Brian Haynes

Visit our website: **group.com**

Unless otherwise indicated, all Scripture quotations are taken from the *Holy Bible* New Living Translation, copyright © 1996, 2004, 2007. Used by permission of Tyndale House Publishers, Inc., Carol Stream, Illinois 60188. All rights reserved.

Library of Congress Cataloging-in-Publication Data

Haynes, Brian, 1973-
  Shift: what it takes to finally reach families today/ by Brian Haynes.
     p. cm.
  ISBN 978-0-7644-3898-1 (pbk. : alk. paper)
1. Family--Religious life. 2. Parenting--Religious aspects--Christianity. 3. Christian education--Home training. 4. Church work with families. I. Title.
  BV4526.3.H39 2009
  248.8'45--dc22
                                  2009020315

10 9 8 7 6   18 17 16 15 14 13 12 11

Printed in the United States of America.

WHAT OTHERS ARE SAYING ABOUT SHIFT

"Brian Haynes gets you in touch with the exciting movement of God to bring the church and families together to spiritually equip this next generation. In *Shift* he gives you the solid, practical ideas we've all been looking for to create a stronger family ministry and transformed lives."

Jim Burns, Ph.D.
President of HomeWord
Author of *Confident Parenting* and
Teaching Your Children Healthy Sexuality

"Wow! This book gets my highest recommendation! *Shift* is a masterful blend of biblical principles, personal transparency, ministry vision, and practical tools. Occasionally a new book comes out with the potential to transform church culture, and this one's got it. Brian Haynes will leave you persuaded that it *is* possible to see a new generation of parents follow the pattern of Deuteronomy 6. This isn't just theory and propositions; Haynes has *done* it in his church, and this book tells you how. The title, *Shift,* isn't just wishful thinking but is prophetic of what will happen to any church leader who dares to read this book!"

Larry Fowler
Executive Director of Global Training for Awana
Author of *Raising a Modern-Day Joseph*

"Church leaders are beginning to realize that what happens at home is more influential than what happens at church, and as a result they're looking for innovative ways to bring Christ and authentic Christlike living back into the center of every household. *Shift* presents one of those innovative, effective, and practical approaches."

Pastor Mark Holmen
National and international consultant and speaker for
the "Faith At Home" movement (faithbeginsathome.com)
Author of *Building Faith at Home*

"Finally! We've searched high and low for a powerful yet practical family ministry strategy that all churches can implement and sustain. Brian Haynes' approach is all that and more! It's biblical and natural for churches and families. It's what you've sensed in your spirit that families need and churches can do."

Christine Yount Jones
Group's Children's Ministry Champion
Executive Editor of Children's Ministry Magazine

"In classes and seminars on family ministry, I repeatedly encourage churches to partner with parents to develop rites of passage that guide children toward Christ-centered maturity. Inevitably, someone asks me, 'But how?' Until now, no outstanding resources have been available to answer that question. In *Shift*, Brian Haynes not only fills that gap but also provides a practical foundation for implementing family-equipping ministry in the local church. *Shift* is, hands-down, the best book of its kind that's available right now. This book needs to find its way into the hands of every minister in your church."

Dr. Timothy Paul Jones
Associate Professor of Leadership and Church Ministry
Editor of The Journal of Family Ministry
Author of *Christian History Made Easy, Misquoting Truth,*
and *Perspectives on Family Ministry*

"The church I preached in yesterday recognized its high school graduates in caps and gowns. The youth pastor leaned over before the service and said, 'I see families of graduates this morning I have not seen in months or years. And look how motivated they are. They wouldn't have missed this moment for anything.' Years ago those same parents were front and center for baby dedication or the baptism of a child. Brian Haynes knows this better than anyone. He's figured out how to capture this unique motivation parents experience at milestone moments—and use it to lead parents into rich training and guidance in family life. Gathering parents at these teachable moments allows churches to enrich marriages, teach parenting, and coach parents toward spiritual leadership in the home. The concept in *Shift* is brilliant, simple, and destined to be reproduced in thousands of churches."

Richard Ross, Ph.D.
Professor of Student Ministry, Southwestern Seminary

"Churches have been talking about the importance of family ministry for more than a decade, but it's surprising how few workable models for actually implementing a family ministry strategy have been created. *Shift* represents a simple-to-understand, pragmatic, and momentum-producing plan that, literally, any church can follow. The cost in time and energy will be dwarfed by the fruits—lifelong followers of Jesus Christ."

Rick Lawrence
Executive Editor of Group Magazine
Co-Author of *The Family-Friendly Church*

"This book is unlike any book you have ever read! *Shift* provides great hope to leaders because it shows, in a practical manner, what a church that truly impacts the family looks like. The milestones presented in *Shift* are not theory to Brian, but have been shaped by enduring truth and a faithful ministry to the Bride of Christ for nearly 15 years."

Steve Wright
Student Pastor
Author of *reThink* and *ApParent Privilege*

"If we're going to reach the next generation for Christ, it has to be through the primary vehicle given by God...the family. If we're going to develop spiritual champions for Christ in our culture, churches and parents must work together to develop a solid plan. Brian Haynes' *Shift* is the book that will catapult ministers and church leaders forward in the cultural battle for families."

Matt Markins
Director and Co-Founder, D6 Conference

"I have seen the impact of the family ministry model launched by Brian Haynes and the Kingsland Baptist Church team and urge church leaders to learn from his vision. Brian has made a great contribution to the emerging movement of Faith@Home churches!"

Kurt Bruner
Executive Director, Strong Families Innovation Alliance

"Brian Haynes knows what he's talking about. His model is biblical and transferable. If you care about the home and the ability of parents to disciple their children, you need to read this book. Pastors, ministry leaders, and parents will all benefit from this great work."

Randy Stinson, Ph.D.
Dean, School of Church Ministries
The Southern Baptist Theological Seminary
President, The Council on Biblical Manhood and Womanhood

To my wife, Angela, the most beautiful, cherished, undeserved gift.
Your beauty astounds me, your friendship excites me, your wisdom comforts me,
and your motherhood is an act of worship that ripples into the generations.

To my daughters—Hailey, Madelyn, and Eden,
Follow us as we follow Jesus.

To the parents raising the boys who will marry my daughters,
Shema!

ACKNOWLEDGMENTS

As with any project of this magnitude, there are people I need to thank for making this book possible. Thanks first to my family for the hours and hours of time you allowed me to write. Specifically, I need to thank my wife, Angela, who has worked tirelessly in ways no one knows but me so that I might write down what we are living out together. It is impossible to separate you from this. Thanks to Mike and Phyllis Haynes and Ed and Mabel Abboud for being faithful, godly parents and grandparents. Thanks to Alex for leading me. Thanks to Doyle for believing and budgeting. Thanks to the Generational Team at Kingsland Baptist Church (Barbara, Vicki, Patrick, and Josh, as well as Paul, Trisha, Mike, and Brian) for your tireless pursuit of legacy and your willingness to follow me. Thank you to the entire pastoral staff at Kingsland. Your willingness to walk the path is amazing. Thank you to the people of Kingsland. You're leading the way in more ways than you can imagine. Keep walking the path of legacy milestones. Thanks to Cynthia, Meredith, Mary Lou, Vicki, and Kathy for reading, editing, and keeping me from looking stupid. It takes a village. Thanks to Todd, Bill, and Marty for kicking me in the pants from the Negev to the Golan Heights. Thanks to Mike Broyles for encouraging me to be persistent. Thanks to Christine Yount Jones at Group for believing. Thanks to the entire team at Group for embracing the message. Most of all thank you, God. You're up to something, and I am grateful to be a small part of it in my generation. May the whole world, throughout the generations, know that you alone are God and may we follow you, Jesus, as our King.

CONTENTS

FOREWORD

Brian Haynes picked the perfect title for this book. At a time of unparalleled changes in our culture, community, and churches, Brian's book captures what I believe is a powerful, positive, and seismic shift.

For years we've poured time and energy into creating outstanding programs and platforms for ministry in the local church. It's my honor to cross the country visiting hundreds of churches, and I've seen the incredible level of quality and excellence in ministry to children. Yet the sad fact is that in spite of all these efforts, we're losing the next generation! Take a room full of second-grade children in a Sunday school class at church today, and then erase seven out of 10 names by the time those children are out of high school. That's the number of children that studies show *won't* be sold-out followers of Christ (or even attending church at all).

The answer to reaching the next generation for Christ isn't better programs. During the one to two hours a week that a family is at church (two or three a times a month), the church is doing lots of great things. But Brian Haynes is right. We must make a shift to equipping parents to become the primary spiritual trainers in their own homes.

We've outsourced the cleaning of our clothes, the washing of our windows, the mowing of our yards—and, unfortunately, we've also outsourced the spiritual training of our children. But that doesn't have to be the case in your home or—if you're a church leader, in the lives of your church families.

Brian Haynes is one of the emerging thought leaders in a small, but exploding group of spiritual formation and family life pastors who have made the shift to equipping parents to take their faith home. I've seen Brian share his Milestone model, and I've seen hands shooting up and people staying late after his presentation was over, just to talk more about the model for faith-transference he's created.

You simply must read this book if you're serious about understanding and implementing a model for equipping parents that can work in your home —and your church—today. It's time for a shift in the way we've been equipping parents, and this book will provide you with a tremendous picture and life-changing plan on how to make that shift successfully.

John Trent, Ph.D.
President, The Center for StrongFamilies and StrongFamilies.com
Author of *The Blessing* and *The 2-Degree Difference*

INTRODUCTION

While driving through my suburban Houston neighborhood of Katy, Texas, a few years ago, I heard the Lord speak very clearly to my heart. Most of the houses here tend to start looking very much alike. Nice lawns and brick exteriors are the norm. As I took in the scenery on my way home at the end of the day, my heart and mind collided with a poignant truth. Behind every generic brick front and beautiful lawn was a unique family. Single moms, empty nesters, the traditional dad and mom with two kids and a dog, people on top of the world, and those drowning in its pain. That was when I felt the impression of the Lord to "reach Katy for Christ…one home at a time."

That's what Brian's strategy does. Brian's book gives a refreshing view of biblical discipleship and the partnership that needs to exist between parents and the local church. Our church encourages parents to be the primary faith influencers of their children. That might imply that the church isn't needed. This is absolutely not the case. It's simply a matter of priorities…parents first and the church second. It's biblical as well as practical. Let me explain.

When Jesus told us in Matthew 22 that the greatest commandment was to love the Lord your God with all your heart and with all your soul and with all your mind, he was quoting an ancient text that says the following:

"Love the Lord your God with all your heart and with all your soul and with all your strength. These commandments that I give you today are to be upon your hearts. Impress them on your children. Talk about them when you sit at home and when you walk along the road, when you lie down and when you get up" (Deuteronomy 6:5-7, NIV).

Do you see the clear progression? We love God. God's words are in our hearts. And we then impress them upon our children's hearts in daily life. The church certainly supports this, but it begins at home. This is why I say it's biblical as well as practical. The average parent has exponentially more time to invest in a child than even the most active church.

So to those reading this book, thank you. We are a work in progress at Kingsland, but we're completely committed to the journey ahead. The next generation and the kingdom of God are worth every effort. I pray the Lord will speak to you as you turn these pages.

Alex Kennedy
Senior Pastor
Kingsland Baptist Church

"For I will speak to you in a parable. I will teach you hidden lessons from our past—stories we have heard and known, stories our ancestors handed down to us. We will not hide these truths from our children; we will tell the next generation about the glorious deeds of the Lord, about his power and his mighty wonders" (Psalm 78:2-4).

Reflection

Not long ago I found myself in a situation that I didn't anticipate experiencing for at least another 20 years. My mom and dad had traveled to Houston from their home nestled in the foothills of the Appalachian Mountains at the base of Pisgah National Forest in Brevard, North Carolina. The visit was anything but a pleasure trip. This time the ominous task that lay ahead overshadowed the excitement of seeing their grandchildren. We made the 45-minute commute from my house to M.D. Anderson Cancer Center on a Monday morning. Our purpose was to receive a clear diagnosis on a suspected brain tumor in the thalamic region of Mom's brain. I wheeled my mother (a woman who only three months earlier regularly hiked miles in the forest and told stories to preschoolers at the public library) into the doctor's office for what would be the appointment of her lifetime. I watched her face as one of the most respected neuro-oncologists in the country explained that Mom had an aggressive, high-grade glioblastoma on her thalamus and brainstem that would be the catalyst for her death. She was only 59 years old.

The plan to begin radiation and chemo to gain a few short months of life shifted into gear. We drove back to my house that night, somber, but hopeful that the radiation treatment would buy precious time. We never made it to the treatment phase.

Over the next three days the tumor surged in its intensity, causing traumatic physical events for my mom that forced emergency admittance to M.D. Anderson. She was in a comatose state and fading quickly. I thought I'd certainly conversed with my mother for the last time. But after surgery to drain fluid off her brain, she popped back into reality, affording us (my dad, brother, and me) the great opportunity to have all the conversations you'd want to have with your wife or mom before she passed away. Though emotionally draining and physically intense, I count these days with my mom as a gift.

My brother, Andy, and I sat in the dark hospital room by Mom's bed, intent on saying goodbye in a way that would matter. We're both pastors with experience in walking people through these kinds of circumstances. It's quite another thing when it's your own mother. Instituting a "no regrets" policy, we poured out our hearts to Mom. We talked about everything from our love of her homemade popsicles when we were kids to the deep spiritual blessing she had always been to us. We thanked her for her guidance, discipline, love, and prayers over the years. We attempted to bless her. Instead, she blessed us.

When we were done talking, Mom presented us with a question. "What was the last Scripture you taught your kids?" she asked in a gentle but expectant voice. Andy responded first, describing something he'd taught Micah and Mia the week before. I honestly don't remember exactly what he said. I was too busy trying to stifle my sobbing. After Andy finished, I told Mom that during the summer I'd been teaching the girls about God through talks about shade, refuge, rock, and living water. Later I realized she was testing her own effectiveness. Were her sons actually teaching her grandchildren the Scripture? Did the importance of parent-to-child faith training make it to the next generation in the Haynes family?

Mom told us how proud she was of us. She told us she wanted those grandkids to become Christian men and women. She mentioned the Shema that I talk about so much. I remember it because she said it in her best North Carolina accent under the influence of narcotics. It came out like "Sheeeeema." It made me laugh in the midst of my tears—but it also caused me to have a light-bulb moment.

My mom thought about the importance of Deuteronomy 6:4-9 before I could even read. She and Dad did their best to impress God's commands on their children. At the end of her life, she wanted to know that her life in

Christ made a difference in her grandchildren's lives. At the end of her day, what mattered to my mom was this spiritual legacy. I am forever grateful, and I pray that her attentiveness to Deuteronomy 6 in the life of her son somehow penetrates your life, your home, and your church.

"Understand, therefore, that the Lord your God is indeed God. He is the faithful God who keeps his covenant for a thousand generations and lavishes his unfailing love on those who love him and obey his commands" (Deuteronomy 7:9).

Starting Out ◀

A Cultural Shift

I'll never forget it as long as I live. I packed up her new pink backpack, tied her shoes, and strapped her into the car seat to take her to school. It was the first day of kindergarten and Hailey, my oldest daughter, was ready to go. I, on the other hand, was a total mess.

As we paraded to school in a long line of cars, I thought about all the things I should've taught her before kindergarten, things like what to do if some boy tries to kiss her at recess or how to pay the lunch lady for milk. When my wife and I escorted Hailey into the classroom, a realization reverberated in my head like a sounding gong. It was so loud I covered my ears: *I have just sent my baby into the world to learn to be like the world.*

In one split second I thought of all the influences that entered my daughter's life in that moment. There was her teacher, someone I didn't know, who would guide her learning every day. Then there were 22 classmates who would be with Hailey eight hours a day. With them came religions, morals, ethics, and values consistent with their families and their cultures. In that one classroom, Buddhism, Hinduism, Judaism, Islam, atheism, and secular humanism were present and accounted for and valued more highly than Christianity. My prayer life deepened dramatically that day as a dad trying to raise a Christ-follower in a world full of lies.

Meet Me at Starbucks

If you and I were to sit down for a cup of coffee and engage in the kind of conversation that goes beyond small talk to what matters, you would find a level of sadness in my heart. Not hopelessness or the absence of joy, but a real sadness for the cause of Christ in Western civilization and a strong belief that we would do well as church leaders to discern the direction of the culture and anticipate its future ramifications.

King David recognized the necessity of understanding the times to plot a strategic course. As David built an army to represent his newly established kingdom, he added to the army "men of Issachar, who understood the times and knew what Israel should do" (1 Chronicles 12:32, NIV). These men helped David establish a culture in Israel that honored God. We too can become men and women who understand the times and know what the church should do to establish a culture that honors God. What is the truth about our times?

Families—The United States has the highest divorce rate among Western countries.[1] Although this rate has remained stable for the last decade, the marriage rate continues to fall.[2] According to the U.S. Census Bureau, of the 73.7 million children younger than 18 in the United States, 67.8 percent live with married parents, 2.9 percent live with two unmarried parents, 25.8 percent live with one parent, and 3.5 percent live with no parent present.[3]

Violence—The U.S. Department of Health and Human Services reports that an estimated 905,000 children were victims of abuse and maltreatment in 2006.[4] An estimated 1,530 child fatalities resulting from abuse or neglect occurred that year.[5] By the time the average child graduates from elementary school, he or she will have watched more than 8,000 murders and more than 100,000 other violent acts on television (the numbers are even higher when homes have cable television).[6]

Teenage Turmoil—Every year in the U.S. almost 750,000 young women ages 15 to 19 get pregnant—an estimated one-third of these pregnancies end in abortion.[7] A 2005 survey of high school students found that 10.8 percent of girls and 4.2 percent of boys, grades 9 to 12, were forced to have sexual intercourse at some time in their lives.[8] In 2004 teen suicides increased at the highest rate in 15 years.[9] By the time teenagers are high school seniors, 38 percent of them have experimented with illegal drugs.[10]

These cold, hard facts reveal the terrifying destruction of the biblical family model in our culture. Why has this moral decline taken place? At its most foundational point, the answer lurks in the belief that everyone has the right to define truth for her- or himself, negating any moral absolute. People make decisions in the moment based on how they feel, not on a standard of truth greater than themselves. The value of individual rights in the family now outweighs the authority God gives to parents. Our culture pays a high price because of this worldview. Children expect the freedom to set their personal boundaries as teenagers, and parents feel as if they have no right to discipline their children. Often, fathers view their lives as their own, not calculating the domino effect of poor choices on their wives and children. Although the culture and the religious community talk about a pro-family and youth-loving society, practices often don't support these claims. Most of the structures of daily life actually pull families apart.

This worldview directly opposes the biblical mandate of the church and Christian life. As a result, the church faces the enormous task of teaching Christ-followers to embrace a relational worldview and leave behind the ingrained individualistic worldview. The difficulty of this task and the current failure of the church in accomplishing this work present a bleak cultural status quo. The tragedy, unless something changes, is that today's children will live a warped, individualistic, self-serving form of Christianity. They'll make decisions based on feelings rather than truth. They'll embrace all philosophies and religions as equally true. They'll teach their children to do the same. And eventually, as life goes by, the influence of Christianity in our culture will grow dim and silent.

What Would It Be Like?

What would it be like? is a question I often ask myself. Not, what would it be like to be a millionaire or a pro athlete? Not, what would it be like to have a perfect life, a perfect job, or a perfect family? My question is more contemplative and calculated than those.

In my mind the over-arching question is "What would it be like if the church of Jesus Christ actually influenced the culture in a biblical way?" Thinking about potential answers to this question yields literally dozens of other questions. What would be different? Would there be less crime and more community? Would there be less divorce and more commitment? Would the moral standard continue to slip, or would it turn in a different direction?

Two questions, though, constantly bang on the doorway of my mind. If the church impacted the culture biblically, would the family be disintegrating? If the church equipped the family spiritually, would the next generation become the greatest generation of Christ-followers ever?

Maybe you are a church planter, a pastor, a children's pastor, a youth pastor, or a discipleship specialist. Maybe you teach third-grade Sunday school, giving hours to help the next generation learn to follow Jesus. Maybe you are on top of the mountain, ready to conquer the world spiritually. Maybe you are in the desert, defeated by the status quo. Maybe you are like me: full of questions.

Are you weary of having the greatest programs in the world while the people and the families around you self-destruct? Maybe you're concerned about the next generation, struggling tirelessly to keep them on the straight and narrow. You wonder how the prevailing culture and the truth of the Bible can actually coexist. I think it's time for a shift.

The great hope for our culture and the families and people living in it is, of course, Jesus Christ. As pastors, ministers, and Christian leaders, we believe this at our core. Sadly, though, we've forgotten one thing. Jesus never said, "Bring your kids to the church so the professionals can lead them spiritually." Rather, the plan from the beginning has been for the church and family to work together for the spiritual formation of the next generation. This book offers a strategy to make the shift that will equip the generations to follow Jesus. Innovative? No way. It's a timeless biblical strategy, revisited because the status quo is unacceptable. What would it be like if every Christian church intentionally and effectively equipped the generations…one home at a time? It would be an undeniable legacy causing a massive cultural shift from the tolerant, humanistic, godless, and compartmentalized present to a radically different, God-honoring future. I think we can do it—but we better do it now.

"He decreed statutes for Jacob and established the law in Israel, which he commanded our forefathers to teach their children, so the next generation would know

them, even the children yet to be born, and they in turn would tell their children. Then they would put their trust in God and would not forget his deeds but would keep his commands" (Psalm 78:5-7, NIV).

NOTES

1. Andrew J. Cherlin "American Marriage in the Early Twenty-First Century;" Marriage and Child Well-being, Vol. 15, No. 2, Fall 2005.

2. "Births, Marriages, Divorces, and Deaths;" National Vital Statistics Reports, Volume 56, No. 12; National Center for Health Statistics, June 2007.

3. "Families and Living Arrangements: 2007;" 2007 Current Population Survey; U. S. Census Bureau.

4. "Child Maltreatment 2006"; Chapter 3: Children; U.S. Department of Health and Human Services.

5. "Child Abuse and Neglect Fatalities"; Child Welfare Information Gateway; The National Child Abuse and Neglect Data System.

6. Bushman, B.J. & Huesmann, L.R., "Effects of Televised Violence on Aggression" in *Handbook of Children and the Media;* Thousand Oaks, CA: Sage Publications, 2001.

7. "U.S. Teenage Pregnancy Statistics"; Guttmacher Institute; updated 2006.

8. "Sexual Violence"; Centers for Disease Control and Prevention; Spring 2008.

9. "Suicide Trends Among Youth and Young Adults Aged 10-24 Years"; Centers for Disease Control and Prevention; 2007.

10. "Trends in the Prevalence of Marijuana, Cocaine, and Other Illegal Drug Use"; Youth Risk Behavior Survey; Centers for Disease Control and Prevention; 2007.

God's Original Blueprint

There are places in the world that reverberate with antiquity. Jerusalem is one such place. As you enter through the Damascus gate into the old city of Jerusalem, you're in the open market of the Muslim quarter. Weaving through the crowded streets you pass shops filled with every kind of commerce imaginable. After what seems like a fairly short distance, you cross into the Jewish quarter and eventually arrive at the Western Wall, one of the holiest places on Earth in the Jewish culture.

Covering your head out of respect and approaching the wall to say a prayer, you immerse yourself in the activity around you. Orthodox Jews wearing phylactery boxes and bindings on their arms murmur prayers, desiring to be closer to God. You look around and notice older men teaching younger men the Scriptures from the Torah. Out of your peripheral vision you catch a glimpse of a father helping his young son memorize words of spiritual formation. You listen, closely intrigued by the beauty of the moment. You hear these words…

Sh'ma Yis'ra'eil Adonai Eloheinu Adonai echad.

V'ahav'ta eit Adonai Elohekha b'khol l'vav'kha uv'khol naf'sh'kha uv'khol m'odekha.
Vhayu had'varim ha'eileh asher anokhi m'tzav'kha
hayom al l'vavekha.
V'shinan'tam l'vanekha v'dibar'ta bam b'shiv't'kha b'veitekha uv'lekh't'kha vaderekh uv'shakh'b'kha uv'kumekha.
Uk'shar'tam l'ot al yadekha v'hayu l'totafot bein einekha.
Ukh'tav'tam al m'zuzot beitekha uvish'arekha.

Suddenly the 21st century and this ancient text, known as the Shema, collide. The child recites the words as his father encourages him. *Those words,* you think to yourself. Strangely familiar and yet so foreign, they constitute the foundation for any biblical strategy of spiritual formation, beginning in Moses' time, confirmed by Jesus himself, and especially relevant in the churches where you and I serve. In English, those words read like this.

"Hear O Israel, the Lord Our God, the Lord is one.
Love the Lord your God with all your heart and with all your soul and with all your strength.
These commandments that I give you today are to be upon your hearts.
Impress them on your children.
Talk about them when you sit at home and when you walk along the road, when you lie down and when you get up.
Tie them as symbols on your hands and bind them on your foreheads.
Write them on the doorframes of your houses and on your gates"
(Deuteronomy 6:4-9, NIV).

Why are these words so important? This is God's plan for the spiritual formation of the generations. You don't have to travel to Jerusalem to unearth God's original plan. The Bible details the plan in all its simplicity. Parents teach their children how to love God by loving God in front of them. Parents intentionally impress the truth of God on their children. Nothing fancy. Beautifully simple.

A Closer Look at the Plan

In the original blueprint the Shema is the foundation plan for effective spiritual formation. Listen closely.

"Hear O Israel, the Lord Our God, the Lord is one."

The Shema begins with a reference point. An undeniable, non-negotiable understanding that there is one God and he alone is God. This is the beginning of spiritual formation. It's the first step of faith. It's the most foundational truth to pass on to the next generation.

"Love the Lord your God with all your heart and with all your soul and with all your strength. These commandments that I give you today are to be upon your hearts."

The second phrase of the Shema tells us as adults and parents of the generations to love the Lord with all our being. God knew that younger generations would need a model of what loving God looks like. So God placed the generations in families to learn from parents how to love God with all their hearts, all their souls, and all their strength. How awesome would it be if all children grew up in homes with parents who passionately loved God in front of them despite the circumstances of life?

Authenticity is a core value of the Shema. God asks people to first have these commands on their hearts before they ever try to pass them down to their children. You and I have seen it all before in ministry. The young people and children we work with often grow in their faith during an extended time away from normal life. Times like camp or missions trip or vacation Bible school. But if they go home to parents who lack an authentic love for God, children will soon be discouraged, and their newfound passion for relationship with God will inevitably diminish. Why? Parents are the primary faith influencers in their children's lives by design. To equip the generations effectively, we must reach and equip parents.

I suppose we should stop and recognize the obvious. As leaders of Christ-followers in whatever community, church, and ministry role we serve, we have the awesome responsibility to model a passionate love for God. Besides your own children, you may think the most important people you live your life in front of are the children or young people you shepherd. Though this is crucial, I'm learning that it's even more important to love God with all of my being in front of their parents. If we model a passionate love for God, parents will begin to model it for their children. This is the way God's spiritual formation strategy works best.

"Impress them on your children. Talk about them when you sit at home and

when you walk along the road, when you lie down and when you get up."

We see the story of life from a very limited perspective. We each see it from our own vantage point, from our little spot on the planet, in our very temporal space in time. God, however, sees the meta-narrative or the greater story that spans generations. He's concerned about how the story of one generation impacts the future of another generation. His desire is for the elder generation to impress the story of God on the younger generation. God gives fathers and mothers the incredible responsibility of telling the younger generation his praiseworthy deeds.

As the Designer of humanity, God knows—and every sane psychologist agrees—that the single most important experience in a person's life is his or her family of origin. Everything flows from the original familial relationships that we enter without choice. God's plan for spiritual formation places the family in the lead when it comes to equipping the next generation. Parents are to impress the commands of God on their children in everyday life as they walk along the road, as they sit at home, when they lie down, and when they get up. This is a lost art among Christians in our culture for various reasons.

Families are busy. Kids participate in extracurricular activities by the time they enter preschool. Teenagers' pressured lives create stress and anxiety. Parents rush around in pursuit of the best for their children and may miss the opportunity to teach God's ways in the natural rhythms of life. There's rarely opportunity to experience God's presence or see God at work. Rest is considered a concept for the weak.

Parents think discipling their children is professionals' job. Most Christian parents' actions reveal their belief that the spiritual growth of their children is primarily the responsibility of trained specialists. Just as parents take their children to soccer practice to be taught by a trained coach, they take their children to church to facilitate spiritual growth. This view is only half true—the church and parents must work together.

Parents aren't sure how to be primary faith influencers. Training a child spiritually seems frightening and foreign to the average parent. Many parents truly have no idea what it looks like to teach their children how to relate to God through the life, death, and resurrection of Jesus. It's rare to find a 30- or

40-something parent who understands the practice of impressing God's commands on their children in daily life. This is a problem that we as church leaders can address. We can revisit the original blueprint and teach parents how to practice the Shema for the sake of the generations.

Where We Walked Off the Path

Why has the typical 21st century church abandoned God's original plan, instead viewing itself as the only vehicle for discipling the generations? This shift is caused by a number of factors.

Many church leaders operate under the erroneous assumption that Old Testament principles are of lesser value than New Testament principles. Church leaders deduce that spiritual formation this side of the resurrection of Jesus Christ occurs through the vehicle of New Testament church alone. This negates the whole counsel of God's Word and perverts God's intentional plan for leading children spiritually. Just because God revealed his redemptive plan through Jesus and established communities, which we now call church, doesn't mean that parents no longer have the primary faith influence.

The church-growth movement redefined success. Beginning in the 1950s the role of the pastor changed from shepherd to growth strategist. Pastors and church leaders attended dozens of conferences and read hundreds of books designed to get more people inside the church facility on Sunday morning. There's measurable value in this; when people come to our churches, we're able to influence them for Christ. But the definition of success in ministry changed from an emphasis on spiritual formation to an emphasis on numeric growth. The church chose events as the preferred vehicle for spiritual formation. We often used gimmicks and guilt to bolster numbers. For most churches by the 1990s, the family didn't even register as a viable vehicle for equipping the generations. We developed children's ministries and youth ministries and gave hired professionals the responsibility for mentoring too many children. In short, we did it our way. We built magnificent organizations, but we produced a version of Christianity that is compartmentalized and humanistic. Our culture is now paying the price for "our version" of Christianity.

Please don't misread me. I'm not anti-church, anti-growth, or anti-conference. I'm simply not in favor of growth strategies that negate God's plan for spiritual formation. The church was never intended to be a substitute for the home. Helping children grow in their relationship with God is a biblical partnership that involves the family and the church.

What Does This Mean for Us as Church Leaders?

God invites us to join him in a shift of seismic proportions. Everywhere I go church leaders are wrestling with the issues of culture, family, and equipping the generations. Everyone is rethinking strategy. Many are asking how we can equip the generations by using family as the primary influencer of kids' spiritual growth. I love to hear these questions. The questions are evidence of God's work in the lives of leaders across the country. God is in this. God will give you the strategy, but first God wants to give you courage.

Courage to Adjust Our Lives

If you and I are to lead our churches to embrace a strategy that engages every Christian home, we must first each evaluate our personal strategy for equipping the next generation living at our own home address. Angela and I have three daughters—Hailey, Madelyn, and Eden. It's our responsibility to love the Lord our God with all our heart and with all our soul and with all our strength in front of them each day. It's our responsibility to keep the words of God on our hearts and impress them on our children. The important question for the people at my church is not, "Does Pastor Brian present a plausible strategy for equipping the generations?" The question of authenticity is, "Does Pastor Brian effectively disciple his own children?"

It's best to ask this question of yourself now and make a course correction if necessary. How are you intentionally leading your children spiritually as a father or mother, not as a ministry leader or pastor? If you're like me, you may realize that your default is to bring your children to church just like everyone else. It's possible that the situation in your home related to equipping the next generation needs strengthening.

I know. I know. All the meetings and people at church consume your time and energy, leaving none for the spiritual formation of your children. Maybe you believe that working hard to make church a life-changing experience is the same thing as helping your children develop spiritually. If you can just lead your church to have the best children's ministry and the best youth ministry, your own children will get everything they need spiritually. You know that isn't true according to Scripture, but often this is the way we practice life. If this is the case, recognize your personal need to adjust your life to God's plan. Make it your priority to become the primary faith influencer of the children living in your home.

Early in my ministry I found myself serving as a student pastor in a local congregation struggling to make a difference for Christ in its community. For a variety of reasons, the church began to decline in attendance. Young families left the church in search of dynamic children's ministries and youth ministries to scratch spiritual itches that our church didn't succeed in alleviating. I was hurt and frustrated. Looking back I am embarrassed to say that in my soul I believed I could work harder to make the church succeed. For the sake of the call on my life to minister in a local church, I put all other priorities on hold, thinking that God wanted me to work harder to make the church a better place.

A couple of years went by. I worked harder and longer, but the church continued its decline. Those two years were damaging and catalytic all at once. Almost every night I'd come home, eat a quick dinner that my wife had prepared, kiss the baby, and head back to church for a meeting. I'd come home exhausted. Angela would already have our daughter in bed, and we'd sit down on the couch to talk. I'd spend the next hour before bed griping about the church I worked so hard to help. This was our family routine for two years.

One night I came home late after an "exhilarating" church council discussion about weighty issues, such as the leaking dishwasher in the church kitchen and the need to pressure wash the molding brick facade. My wife and I talked about church once again. This time the conversation went in a completely different direction.

As I babbled about my frustrations related to church, I heard these words: "You are losing us."

I listened. My wife told me she felt like a single mom. The man she married was now married to the church. My daughter's father cared more about shepherding other people than teaching her Bible stories at night before she went to bed. Angela, in her patience, had waited two years, hoping I'd figure this out on my own. Now, led by the Holy Spirit, she told me the truth about myself. She asked for change. I was devastated.

Today I'm so glad Angela had the courage to communicate honestly with me. That one conversation jolted me to the core. I reconnected with the truth of Scripture and God's priorities for my life. This meant life change for me. I sought the Lord and God showed me Deuteronomy 6:4-9. I began to well up with passion for my wife and children. I soon saw my kids' spiritual growth as beginning in my home, not the church. I begged God in prayer for a fresh start. God orchestrated a career move to allow me the balance I needed to be a Christ-follower, a husband, a father, and then a pastor.

One night soon after we moved, my daughter Hailey, four years old at the time, looked up from her plate and asked, "Dad, what are you doing home for dinner?" With tears in my eyes I promised her I'd be home for dinner most nights from that point forward. Now family dinners, regular Faith Talks, celebrations, and God Sightings characterize our family life because of prioritized time and a plan to equip our daughters to become Christ-followers. Out of the overflowing life of my family comes the heart of my ministry. I can authentically expect our church to pursue parent-based spiritual formation because of the foundation of Scripture and the real experience of my own family.

Family Ministry:
A Shift in Strategy

Even Jesus matured through a planned strategic process for spiritual formation. Luke 2:52 reveals that Jesus grew over time, in favor with God and people. In his humanity, the Messiah walked a common path that everyone in Israel understood: Torah, Shabbat, synagogue, sacrifice, the temple, and the commanded observances of Passover, the Feast of Unleavened Bread, the Feast of First Fruits, Shavuot, Rosh Hashanah, Yom Kippur, and Sukkot. Along this path of growth described in the Old Testament, family and religion were not mutually exclusive. In fact, they were inseparable.

Today we need this common path for church and home. Several months after God "reprioritized my life," using the words of my wife, I searched for help as a father, not as a pastor. I stumbled across a book called *Spiritual Milestones* by Jim and Janet Weidmann and Otis and Gail Ledbetter that enlightened me. I saw a way to grow as a father who wanted to lead his daughters spiritually.

Months later I began to think. *What if the discipleship process at church and parents' effort to lead their children spiritually became one simple, common path? What if the church embraced a strategy to equip parents to be the primary faith influencers, giving them motivation, resources, training opportunities, and most importantly a clear path to walk on? What if the church offered Bible study and events that reinforced the parent's role?* These simple thoughts became the beginning of a strategy designed to help my church and its families "equip the generations one home at a time."

Cookie Cutters Are for Cookies

Let me make a clarifying statement. What I am about to show you is a strategy designed specifically for Kingsland Baptist Church in suburban Houston, Texas. The strategy flows naturally from our unique mission, vision, and culture as a church. The principles behind this strategy are universal. It doesn't matter how big or small, old or new, rich or poor, urban or rural; the foundational principles supporting this strategy will work in your church. God is all about linking church and home to equip the generations in every context. However, your church is different from mine. Ours has a style all its own and so does yours. You're the expert regarding your church and your ministry. God most likely has unique tweaks to make in your church to best equip parents and leaders in your context. Your strategic path must be biblical and it must fit your context, but it doesn't have to be just like ours. In fact, while the ideal situation is a churchwide commitment, you may be the lone advocate. If you're a children's or youth ministry leader in this situation, take heart in knowing that you can begin within your ministry area, equipping families and initiating age-appropriate milestones. You can do this even if you have to do it one milestone at a time.

Defining the Terms

It's important to understand the basic terminology associated with this strategy. I'd hate to be the guy who babbles about how to do something using insider terms that most people don't understand. Take a moment to gain a working understanding of each of the following terms.

Milestone—Our strategy focuses on seven milestones that every person growing in his or her relationship with Christ experiences and celebrates. These milestones serve as markers of progression on the spiritual formation journey. When a person reaches a milestone, that growth is celebrated as praise for how God is working in the person and as motivation to continue walking the path.

Core Competencies—Each child, adolescent, or adult must learn key truths as he or she progresses from one milestone to the next. Our church develops leaders in children's and youth ministry who understand the core competencies and can effectively teach them. Our church also works to instill the truths of these core competencies into parents through our adult discipleship ministry. Core competencies represent what we teach in the time between each milestone. We don't limit our teaching to just these principles, but when the core competencies come up, for example, during the course of a Bible study, we highlight them as truth associated with a given milestone.

If a child or young person doesn't learn how to practically apply the core competencies in an age-appropriate way, he or she hasn't yet reached the next milestone.

Faith Talks—Every parent must reinforce the core competencies to his or her children in formal and informal ways. The formal way to teach the core competencies between each milestone in our strategy is called Faith Talks. We define Faith Talks as intentional times set aside each week for conversation based on Scripture. For some this looks very much like family devotions around the kitchen table. For others this is a walk to the park, a trip to Starbucks, or other creative times together.

Every family's Faith Talk style is unique, but Faith Talks are defined by intentionality. Parents set aside a specific time for Faith Talks as a weekly event on every person's calendar. Parents keep core competencies in mind and intentionally plan conversations that help their children move toward the next milestone. On the church side of the equation, we intentionally train and resource parents to lead effective Faith Talks at home.

In 2004 our church contracted with Family Life Ministry in Little Rock, Arkansas, to do a family needs survey. The extensive survey completed by 1,009 adults yielded telling results: Only 17 percent of the parents completing the survey participated in family devotions with any degree of regularity. When it came down to it, our core leadership, who were also parents, didn't take the initiative to lead family devotions even once a week. In 2004 as we began the process of strategic redesign, we realized parents would have to learn how to lead Faith Talks, and they'd have to commit to doing them at least once every week. We now place a lot of effort into motivating and teaching parents to lead a weekly Faith Talk, and we work hard to train them for the task.

God Sightings—God Sightings give parents the opportunity to teach core competencies in informal ways by modeling and speaking truth. These God-orchestrated moments are the things that happen in life as we walk along the road, as we lie down, and as we get up. The art of capitalizing on a God Sighting is fundamental to leading a child spiritually.

We've experienced many memorable God Sightings with our kids. One of the strongest came in 2007 with the birth of our daughter, Eden. Four months into the pregnancy, and while I was on the other side of the planet, Angela went into pre-term labor. After a successful emergency surgery, Angela's doctor prescribed five months of strict bed rest, and the girls and I faced a learning curve. I fixed hair and picked outfits, situations I'd describe as Dante's 7th level of the Inferno. As a family we had to work together to give Mom the time she needed to have a healthy baby. When I use the term *anxious*, it's an understatement. Taking Mom out of the lineup was difficult, but the anxiety of not knowing whether the baby would make it to a safe development point was excruciating. My older daughters prayed for Mommy and baby Eden every night, unprompted, for five months. At the end of the day, we rested in the refuge of God. On June 26, 2007, Eden Katalina was born six weeks early. She came home with us from the hospital 48 hours later.

The week after we brought her home, I pulled out my journal. We sat around the table for what seemed like hours, listing the many ways God had answered our prayers and provided for us. The girls recalled their favorite meals church members had delivered to our house three times a week for five months. Angie recalled the doctors and nurses who not only cared for us but also prayed for us. I remembered all the people who stopped me in the blurriest season of my life to let me know they were praying. I remembered the pastors on our staff taking up the slack for me at work so I could be home more. Of course, as we recounted all this, little Eden snuggled in her mother's arms, the visual representation of God's mercy and grace to the Haynes' family. My girls will remember learning about the faithfulness of God in the desert of "bed rest." Of course, Eden literally means "delight" in Hebrew. We believe that God delighted in our dependence during a difficult time.

God Sightings can be big or small. Watching a baptism on Sunday morning and talking with your child about the meaning of baptism is a God Sighting. Experiencing a sunset together as God's artwork is a God Sighting. When your child asks you how you became a Christian…that's a God

Sighting. Your child catching you in personal prayer or Bible study is a God Sighting. Forgiveness is a God Sighting. Laughter is a God Sighting. They go on and on.

Church Events—Our church hosts events that support the milestones, such as vacation Bible school or a fall festival. Often these events function to assist parents in teaching their children the core competencies leading up to a milestone. We also use church events to celebrate certain spiritual milestones in a big way with other families in the church. Our purpose is to connect parents with each other for support, ideas, and encouragement and to celebrate God's work in children's lives.

Parent Summit Conference—Twice a year, we host a Parent Summit that includes a speaker who has a passion for encouraging and motivating parents and grandparents. We help parents chart their course and determine where their children are on the journey along the milestones path. We also offer all the parent seminars related to the milestones. We view this event as the most important training event in the life of our church each semester.

Parent Seminars—We offer specific seminars related to each milestone, which are designed to equip parents to lead their children toward the next milestone of spiritual development. In most cases a parent needs to attend a parent seminar one to two years before the child or teenager will reach the associated milestone. The parent seminars, led by parents or staff members with expertise, provide important information regarding what parents can expect from children in all aspects of life in the near future and how best to lead them as they grow. Parents who attend parent seminars gain the most from the partnership alignment between the ministry of the church and the ministry of the home.

Q&A ▶

What Do Parents Learn at Parent Seminars?

Every parent seminar covers the following areas so parents walk away feeling equipped and supported.

▶ How the core competencies are experienced at home in the coming months on the way to the future milestone.

▶ How to lead age-appropriate Faith Talks and discover resources to help them do so.

▶ How the church will partner with them to equip them biblically and help them grow as their child's primary faith influencer.

▶ How the children's ministry or youth ministry will partner with them to help their children learn the core competencies.

Family Celebrations—We teach parents how to host at-home celebrations for almost every milestone. The family celebrations assist parents in leading their children to learn a final truth in reaching a given milestone. The family celebrations also function to celebrate what the child has already learned and to reinforce God's work in the life of the child or teenager. In the context of family celebrations, parents often give their children symbolic gifts. For many families these celebrations are the most moving and meaningful steps along the way.

Take-Home Sunday—We use this concept borrowed from Mark Holmen, pastor of Ventura Missionary Church and author of *Building Faith at Home* (Regal), four times a year. On Take-Home Sunday we teach people in adult Bible study groups a specific skill related to leading children through the milestones. Our first Take-Home Sunday focused on God Sightings. In our adult Bible study groups, we defined God Sightings by teaching the Deuteronomy 6 principle of talking about the things of God as we walk along the road, as we lie down, and as we get up. We taught our adults to pray for God Sightings, to pray for the wisdom to recognize God Sightings, and to constantly study the Scripture so they will know how to speak into a child's life as God Sightings occur. We gave each person a stress ball that was shaped like a water drop and labeled "God Sightings." Josh, our adult discipleship pastor, wrote a wonderful lesson about each God Sighting being a drop in the well of a child's spiritual formation experience (see pages 133-135). Since that day I've been in countless homes where I've noticed the stress balls prominently displayed as reminders to seize these God Sightings.

Take-Home Sunday allows us to teach a skill and highlight the strategy with all our adults at least once a quarter. Our philosophy is simple. We use existing vehicles with a lot of momentum, like adult Bible study or small groups, to equip parents. Just a side note: Don't replace regular Bible studies with milestone information more than four times a year. Parents need to be actively engaged in the study of God's Word.

Generational Team—*Team* is the most important term to learn regarding a strategy linking church and home. It will take a team to work this plan. If your church has a staff of discipleship specialists related to age groups, they should be a part of the generational team. Common ministry positions associated with a generational team are children's pastors, youth pastors, adult discipleship pastors, and others who focus on equipping a particular generation of people in the church. You can also draw the generational team from a completely volunteer staff. Churches not paying a plethora of staff members may have a key volunteer leader in each of the generational ministries of the church. The generational team is led by the person responsible for the oversight of the entire spiritual formation ministry of your church. A perfect candidate to lead this team is a family pastor, a discipleship pastor, or the more traditional minister of education. In the case of the smaller church without a discipleship pastor, the senior pastor should lead the generational team.

The purpose of the generational team is to align the children, youth, and adult ministries along a common path of spiritual formation that links church and home and develops ways to equip parents as primary faith influencers.

If you're one person launching this strategy within one ministry area, begin to develop a team that will help you implement the parent training and milestones that relate to the age group you minister to. God will build a team around this important first step.

The Path of Milestones

As parents, Angela and I needed a simple step-by-step approach to becoming the primary faith influencers for our daughters. Even more so, we needed the church to partner with us in the spiritual development of our children—not to take our place as the primary faith influencers, but to train us and to reinforce what we're teaching our children. At our church and in our home, we refer to this strategic partnership as the action of "walking the path of legacy milestones." This path allows the next generation to experience a congruent growth and development pattern at church and home. This user-friendly path is designed to be traveled one small step at a time. As a church leader, walk with me now along the path of milestones.

Milestone 1 ◀

Milestone 1: The Birth of a Baby

"Then it was time for their purification offering, as required by the Law of Moses after the birth of a child; so his parents took him to Jerusalem to present him to the Lord" (Luke 2:22).

Church Leader:	Preschool minister, volunteer preschool leader, or children's pastor
Parent Seminar:	First Steps (required two-hour seminar)
Church Event:	Parent Commitment Ceremony
Core Competency:	The parent as the primary faith influencer

Milestone 1: What It's All About

Christian parents are naturally compelled to dedicate their newborn children to God. The act of dedication is actually a commitment on the parents' part to raise their child in the ways of the Lord. Taking our cue from the Bible, we lead parents to celebrate Milestone 1: The Birth of a Baby.

This milestone connects new parents with the magnificent responsibility and opportunity of leading their children spiritually. When parents present their children to God, even as Mary and Joseph did, they're acknowledging two simple facts. First, this new baby is God's creation and therefore God's possession. Second, as stewards of God's possession, parents have the responsibility to intentionally raise the child in a way that's pleasing to God.

Strategically, Milestone 1 is all about connecting with parents in a natural season of excitement, curiosity, and perhaps even anxiety, to show them the milestone road map for leading their children spiritually. This is a time of life when parents are looking for help. They leave the hospital with a few pamphlets and no idea about how to raise their new baby. They need God, community, and a plan to do it right. We use Milestone 1 to introduce parents to God's desire to walk with them through this journey called parenting. We demonstrate our commitment as a church to embrace the new family in community and partner with them all along the way in the child's process of spiritual development.

Milestone 1 Champion

In our setting, the preschool minister is our resident Milestone 1 expert. She does the work of connecting families who are expecting a child or have just had a child—either through birth or adoption—to the Milestone 1 process. Not everyone has a preschool minister, though. Possibly you have a children's pastor who works with kids from infancy through fifth grade or a family pastor who oversees spiritual development from infancy to senior adulthood. Maybe you have a volunteer children's ministry coordinator overseeing the children's ministry area. Whoever is the recognized key influencer over families in this stage of life should lead the Milestone 1 process. The idea is to find the person who's passionate about ministry to families and has the influence in the church to lead parents. For us, that person is our preschool minister. For you it might be someone else. To make it easier to communicate, I'll call this key leader the Milestone 1 Champion.

The Milestone 1 Champion works to build relationships with new parents who are eager to influence their children's faith. The preschool ministry hosts the First Steps seminar, coordinates the church event, and discovers or develops resources to help parents. The Milestone Champion's job is to partner with parents in the early phases of spiritual development, preparing parents for the ceremony at church and for the work of faith training at home on the path to Milestone 2.

Milestone 1 Parent Seminar: First Steps

The First Steps seminar is a prerequisite for participating in the church ceremony. Why require the seminar? Without a clear understanding of what it means to be a primary faith influencer, parents commit to a position of responsibility knowing little or nothing about the job description. It's wrong to ask parents in a formal ceremony before a crowd of people to lead their children spiritually without ever teaching them what the Bible says about impressing God's truth on the next generation. New parents typically want information and will enthusiastically attend the seminar to learn how to effectively fulfill the commitment they're making.

Unlike the other milestones, Milestone 1 focuses almost completely on the parents' development. Milestone 1 has only one core competency: The parent is the primary faith influencer. At the parent seminar, new parents learn what it means to live this core competency. We highlight our biblical interpretation of the theology underlying this milestone and children's faith training. Parents get to look at the big picture and the desired destinations along the path at the beginning of the journey. They discover the intentional ways the church will partner with them and equip them to disciple their children. We also discuss children's physical, spiritual, and emotional development from infancy to kindergarten. We give parents information they can use immediately, and we offer them a plethora of effective tools and resources.

Milestone 1
'First Steps' Topics
▶ Parents as primary faith influencers
▶ Understanding the church ceremony
▶ Baby's amazing brain
▶ Parents' influence on developmental areas of growth
▶ Baby's first year
▶ The importance of Dad
▶ The importance of Mom
▶ Ways to bless your child
▶ Ways to pray for your child
▶ First steps toward faith
▶ Milestone 1 resources for families

Milestone 1 Church Event

Once parents attend the required seminar for Milestone 1, they're eligible to participate in their baby's dedication in worship. It's beautiful to watch as the parents, who understand the magnitude of their commitment, vow to lead their children spiritually. In this ceremony, the entire church and the parents agree to work together for the spiritual development of the new babies.

Much like a wedding, the congregation is invited to witness as parents make their commitment. Our pastor introduces each parent and baby to the congregation by showing a digital picture of the baby on the big screens in our worship center. As he introduces the baby, he reads the biblical meaning of the baby's name or a relevant Scripture that relates to the name and offers a blessing, presenting the family with a certificate and a small gift. We often give parents a resource to help them learn to pray for their children or bless their children. (The Milestone 1 Champion organizes all this information for the pastor's use in the ceremony.)

Using Deuteronomy 6:4-9 as the model for the ceremony, parents are asked four questions. "Will you choose this day to live with the commands of God on your own hearts?" "Do you accept responsibility as your child's primary faith influencer to impress the truth and love of God on her as you live life together?" "Will you love this child with the unconditional love of Christ?" "Will you pray for her to know Jesus Christ as her Lord and Savior?" Parents answer, "We do" as a response to each question.

The pastor then turns and asks the congregation, "Will you partner with these parents by praying for them as they lead their children spiritually?" "Will you partner with these parents by teaching their children at church and modeling a Christlike lifestyle in support of what the parents are teaching and modeling?" The congregation answers, "We do" in response to each question. Suddenly the family and the church gain perspective on the order of things. Parents take the lead in the spiritual development of a child. The church equips, trains, and supports parents along the way. This is Milestone 1, the beginning of the path.

Q&A ▶

Where Do New Families Enter the Path?

Parents and children who are new to your church simply jump in where they are—for example, if the family includes older children, this might mean Milestone 4 or 5.

▶ ## Stories Along the Path

Kids on Loan

We attended Parent Summit and the Milestone 1 parent seminar in order to dedicate our second daughter, Avery. It reminded me of pre-marriage counseling, which helps us consider all the facets of a marriage relationship. The seminar reminded us to focus on our daughters' spiritual lives, and the discussion of practical issues helped to reinforce our priorities. The actual commitment service was our public profession that we're committed to raising our daughters in a Christ-centered way. We felt it carried the same weight as our public profession of faith in Christ. In the midst of our friends and church family, we voiced our desire to ensure that our daughters grow up knowing and loving Christ. Also the dedication assured us we're not alone in the journey of raising our family spiritually. We specifically committed to pray for our children. The dedication reminded us that God has loaned us our children and we have the responsibility to return them by making certain they know God's Word. —THE WHITE FAMILY

A Great First Step

It may seem difficult to implement the entire milestone strategy all at once—for many reasons. Maybe time and resources make it impossible initially. Perhaps others in your church leadership hold fast to a philosophy of ministry that continues to overlook the family strategically. In any case, don't let frustration pull you off course.

If all you can do right now is Milestone 1, it's a great place to start because parents discover their God-given responsibility to lead their child spiritually at the very beginning of their child's life. You'll provide parents with tools and resources to help them during their child's most formative years. You'll make sense of the ceremony in your tradition, which parents often misunderstand. You'll help parents learn to lead their children spiritually by teaching them to pray for and with their children, capitalize on God Sightings along the way, and to recognize and celebrate certain spiritual milestones even if your church doesn't formally recognize those milestones in its strategic practice. You'll find that parents will look to you for guidance from infancy into the early elementary years—or longer—when you invest in them at Milestone 1.

Milestone 2 ◀

Milestone 2:
Faith Commitment

"Let the children come to me. Don't stop them! For the kingdom of God belongs to those who are like these children. I tell you the truth, anyone who doesn't receive the kingdom of God like a child will never enter it" (Mark 10:14-15).

Church Leader:	Children's pastor or volunteer children's leader
Parent Seminar:	Leading Your Child to Christ
Church Event:	Faith Commitment Ceremony
Family Celebration:	Spiritual Birthday Party
Core Competencies:	Jesus, faith, the Bible, sin, repentance, salvation

Milestone 2: What It's All About

Children growing up in the context of a Christian family and a Christ-centered church are likely to make a public affirmation to follow Jesus when they're between the ages of 7 and 13. Between Milestone 1 and Milestone 2, parents lead their children toward a relationship with Jesus—quite a journey when you think about it. During this time parents initiate Faith Talks to teach the core competencies, capitalize on God Sightings, and pray like crazy for their son or daughter. This path requires work, persistence, and intentionality.

Milestone 2 Champion

In our church, the children's pastor leads the Milestone 2 process. In other churches this may be a volunteer children's ministry coordinator. In any case the person responsible for children's ministry at your church becomes the Milestone 2 Champion.

There are several key components of the champion's role in the milestone process. First, this person must ensure that the core competencies for Milestone 2 are being taught in age-appropriate children's classes. For a child to understand enough to make an authentic commitment, he or she must learn and understand several key truths. In our church, these core competencies include Jesus, faith, the Bible, sin, repentance, salvation, and baptism. Strategically, while the parent reinforces these core competencies through Faith Talks, the church teaches the same competencies through Sunday school, so the champion pays careful attention to choosing a supportive curriculum.

Kids in first through fifth grade learn biblical truth for practical application, especially in regard to the identified core competencies. We study loads of Bible stories, but the Milestone Champion ensures trained volunteer leaders explain the core competencies for Milestone 2 in an effective and age-appropriate manner. In this way, we lay a scriptural foundation in each child's life that echoes the truth reinforced at home by the parent.

Second, the Milestone Champion becomes the "go to" person for parents who are leading their children toward faith in Jesus. This is important work. The champion communicates the core competencies of Milestone 2 to parents in a variety of ways. Our Milestone Champion publishes a monthly devotion calendar for parents with kids in this growth season, consisting of verses and talking points that support the important core competencies. She's constantly reading, reviewing, and recommending new resources for parents to use as Faith Talk helps. This is crucial. Pointing motivated parents to the proper resources and making those resources available through a library or a resource center allows the church and the family to align on a common path of spiritual formation.

Finally, our Milestone Champion also spends a lot of time meeting with parents and kids about the commitment to follow Christ. She has the opportunity to encourage parents who have taken the lead as the primary faith influencers and to reinforce the child's faith commitment. She gets to weigh motives. Is this child trying to please Mom or Dad or friends, or is this child making a genuine commitment based on an understanding of Jesus, sin, repentance, and salvation? In this way families are shepherded at a very crucial milestone.

Milestone 2 Parent Seminar: Leading Your Child to Christ

Perhaps the most formal way the Milestone Champion equips adults to lead their children spiritually is her work in developing, teaching, and hosting a seminar in support of parents preparing to lead their children toward Milestone 2. The Leading Your Child to Christ seminar is offered twice a year at the Parent Summit. At the seminar, parents learn how to lead Faith Talks highlighting the core competencies. We give parents an understanding of the theology underlying this milestone and place a special emphasis on helping parents recognize that God has a unique plan for each child. Parents with the best motives sometimes rush their children. Desiring to check off the next box, celebrate the next milestone, and move forward on the path, parents get ahead of God. Instead we teach parents to watch for certain signs indicating the work of the Holy Spirit in their children's lives. Are the children relentlessly asking questions? Have you observed them authentically repenting in situations where they disobeyed? Do you see genuine conviction in their lives when they sin? We help parents learn how to balance teaching their children about God's plan for salvation with allowing the Holy Spirit to minister to their children and draw them to Jesus.

Milestone 2
'Leading Your Child to Christ' Topics
▶ Milestone 2 at a glance
▶ Is my child ready?
▶ God's plan of salvation
▶ Friendship with God begins at home
▶ What should my child know about God?
▶ Making a commitment to follow Christ
▶ Planning the Spiritual Birthday Party
▶ Milestone 2 resources for families

▶ ## God Sightings

A Hungry Heart

I was traveling with my two boys, who were hungry and wanted to stop at a McDonald's. As we exited the freeway, we saw an older homeless man near the side of the road. My 8-year-old son Tyler said, "Let's take that man something to eat." I immediately felt afraid and vulnerable and said, "That's a great idea, but Dad wouldn't want us to stop because it isn't safe." As I pulled in to order our food, I saw that Tyler had big tears coming down his cheeks. When I asked him what was wrong, he replied, "What good is an idea if that's all it ever is?" He actually said those exact words as a third-grader. Needless to say, I ordered extra food. In that moment the Holy Spirit revealed to me that I'd been trying to teach my son the importance of compassion but it was more important to show it. —THE STEPHENS FAMILY

Milestone 2 Church Event

Before the ceremony begins, the pastor introduces the children and parents and speaks to the church. Your pastor can say something like this: "We have the incredible opportunity to celebrate an important faith milestone with these families this morning," and then explain the theological framework of the ceremony. In our tradition, we explain, "Baptism is a picture of a changed life in Jesus Christ. As these people are baptized this morning, they're publicly professing their new identity and faith in Jesus for the forgiveness of sin. For each of them, this is a milestone, representing their growth along the path of spiritual formation and of their new life in Christ."

We remind each person in attendance at our church of the milestone process. This intentional wording is important because it connects people with the progression of spiritual formation and our strategy at Kingsland to equip the generations one home at a time. We make a DVD of each baptism and give it to the person being baptized as a reminder of this milestone.

Q&A ▶

What If I'm Older When I Make a Commitment to Follow Christ?

Whether people follow Christ at age 15 or 85, they're experiencing Milestone 2. We celebrate with them at church and thank God for this milestone in their lives. Then we usher adults directly to Milestone 7 so they learn to live as Christ-followers. If they're parents, we introduce them to the rest of the strategy so they can lead their children along the path of milestones.

Milestone 2 Family Celebration

Parents learn to host a family celebration called a Spiritual Birthday Party to commemorate a child's commitment to Christ. Every family's celebration is unique, but each includes common elements. First, the child receives a symbol. Parents give necklaces, bracelets, charms, shields, Bibles, or other personally meaningful symbols that depict the life of faith in Christ. Family, friends, or spiritually influential adults are often invited to celebrate at the spiritual birthday party. Recently I heard of a spiritual birthday party where Sunday school teachers and extended family wrote letters to the child, reflecting on the child's journey toward Christ and the journey ahead. Though the child may not fully appreciate these letters now, they'll become priceless treasures highlighting the partnership of family and church in the child's spiritual life.

Two years ago when my oldest daughter, Hailey, was baptized, we hosted a family celebration that was a "hybrid" spiritual birthday party. We asked her to choose her favorite restaurant. We eat at home most of the time, so eating out is viewed as a special occasion. Then we invited extended family to join us for a time of celebration. Grandparents, cousins, aunts, and uncles showed up to speak into Hailey's life and affirm the decision she'd made to follow Christ. Angela and I presented Hailey with a symbol, a sterling silver shield of faith on a leather strap. Just yesterday as she was leaving for school, I noticed her shield of faith proudly worn around her neck. I smiled because I know whenever she puts it on she remembers her commitment to follow Jesus. The presentation of a symbol in the context of a family celebration has lasting significance and solidifies the distinct purpose of the milestone in the child's spiritual development.

Stories Along the Path

The Power of One Parent

This story is about my 10-year-old son Dustin and his walk through the milestones. We came to Kingsland about three and a half years ago as a single parent family. When I went to the first Parent Summit meeting two years ago, I was a bit overwhelmed by all the different milestones. I started thinking, "We've missed the first milestone already. How on earth could I ever help my son through the rest of these because he doesn't get to always come with me every Sunday?" "How would I ever be strong enough in my own walk with the Lord to lead him?"

Well, some time has passed, and I've grown in my spiritual walk and moved into a leadership role in my Bible study group, and my son has grown and matured in his walk with the Lord. By the grace of God and lots of prayer, learning from my example, and being in his own Bible study class at Kingsland, Dustin was baptized in April of this year, the second Milestone.

I've learned not to doubt God's great and awesome power, and I realize God's hand is in every part of our lives. I may think Dustin isn't watching me, but he is, just as all kids see what their parents do. I've also learned that I can be the spiritual leader of our household and that I can be a good role model for him, no matter what our family situation may be. I know that I can lead my son toward the next milestone with confidence and perseverance, with God right there by our side. Even though Dustin may not have the perfect parents, he most definitely has a perfect Father in heaven, who watches over him and loves him very much, just as God does all of us.

—THE WILLIAMS FAMILY

Milestones 1 + 2 = Foundational Impact

Never underestimate what you can accomplish with these first two milestones, especially if you're the only ministry leader in your church implementing this strategy. When you equip parents and partner with them for the first 11 years or more of their children's lives, you give these families a huge gift. Parents will learn how to lead intentional Faith Talks, recognize God Sightings, and celebrate milestones in their children's spiritual development. You'll offer parents tools, knowledge, and spiritual direction along the way. You'll not only give children the best church experience possible, but you'll also have invested in the most important experience in any person's life—his or her family. My guess is that you'll become a hero or heroine to parents who already sensed they should be leading their children spiritually but didn't know how. Go for it, my friend. You'll find that the stories pouring out from your children's ministry just may influence the strategic direction of your entire church. Certainly you'll have a foundational impact in the lives of every child and family touched by your ministry.

Milestone 3 ◀

Milestone 3:
Preparing for Adolescence

"Don't let anyone think less of you because you are young. Be an example to all believers in what you say, in the way you live, in your love, your faith, and your purity" (1 Timothy 4:12).

Church Leader:	Children's pastor or youth pastor
Parent Seminar:	Preparing for Adolescence
Church Event:	4th and 5th Grade Retreat
Family Celebration:	Road Trip
Core Competencies:	Identity in Christ, spiritual growth, spiritual disciplines

Milestone 3: What It's All About

The church partners with parents to help children between the ages of 9 and 12 prepare spiritually, emotionally, and physically for adolescence. This stage of development requires parents to rethink how they connect with their children relationally to lead them spiritually.

Our kids are growing up too fast. As Christian parents we have the responsibility to equip our children with a strong sense of God's truth to deal with many unavoidable issues in our culture. Isolationism, though appealing, isn't the answer. Instead of protecting our children from the outside in, we need to strengthen them from the inside out. Milestone 3 is all about giving parents the tools to lead their children spiritually through the tumultuous years of adolescence.

It would be easy to make this milestone all about combating the perversion of sex that our culture is so fixated on. That focus isn't broad enough, though, to help children develop the biblical foundation needed to make good decisions. Instead we choose to focus first on identity in Christ as a core competency. Why start here? Understanding our identity in Christ answers two questions that are important for every person to answer. Who am I—and whose am I? As a father I believe the answer to these questions will determine how my daughters deal with the issues of our 21st century culture as teenagers and young adults. Understanding that our identity is in Christ has serious ramifications. First, if I answer the question, "Who am I?" by understanding that I am a free child of Christ, saved by grace, and created with purpose, according to Scripture, then I have identity. I identify with Christ and his way of living life. Second, if I answer the question "Whose am I?" by understanding that as a free child of Christ, saved by grace, and created with purpose, I was bought with a price, then I realize I'm not my own. I'm in community with God and others, and my actions flow out of my identity.

This is a deep biblical truth. I gave my life to Christ and I am fully his. A 9-, 10-, and 11-year-old can understand this when it's taught in Faith Talks at home and in Bible study at church, especially when parents model this in their lives. Identity serves as the necessary base for practical discussions about real issues in preparation for adolescence. Equipping parents to have comfortable, biblically informed conversations with their kids about uncomfortable topics isn't easy. But we must give parents the encouragement, resources, and skills they need to discuss developing bodies, emotional changes, and sex, as well as our culture's perversions of God's gifts. All of this relates to a proper understanding of identity in Christ.

We also partner with parents to teach children at this age the core competencies of spiritual growth and spiritual discipline. These concepts are important. If a child reads the Bible regularly, he will hear the voice of God. If a child prays, she will find wisdom, direction, refuge, forgiveness, and community with God.

Many parents find this challenging. More than once I've been asked, "How can I teach my child to do something I'm not doing myself?" Parents must be pursuing spiritual growth and exercising spiritual discipline as an outpouring of their identity in Christ to influence their children to do the same. This is why a strong adult Christian education ministry is so important.

Milestone 3 Champion

The children's pastor usually owns Milestone 3 as the resident expert. In our church, because of trust and alignment, our student pastor also addresses this milestone. In your church this might be a dedicated children's ministry leader or a spiritually mature parent. As with the other milestones, this Milestone Champion's job is to equip parents to have intentional Faith Talks, work with God Sightings, and use recommended resources to lead their children to embrace the truths of Milestone 3.

Milestone 3 Parent Seminar: Preparing for Adolescence

We encourage parents to attend this seminar before their children turn 9 years old, because engaging children around the core competencies of Milestone 3 is a two-year process. All parents have the responsibility along this section of the path to lead their children to understand their identity in Christ, promote their spiritual growth, and teach and model the spiritual disciplines.

At the parent seminar, parents learn the core competencies and the basics of helping kids navigate relevant issues, such as physical changes, identity in Christ, and sex. We provide resources to help parents lead Faith Talks and capitalize on God Sightings. Parents discover how the church will partner with them so they can intentionally lead their children to become Christlike teenagers. Parents also learn to host family celebrations that serve as catalysts for meaningful conversations with their children.

The beauty of Milestone 3 lies in the extent to which the family and the church work together to help children prepare spiritually and emotionally for adolescence. So often kids have to work through all of this on their own without a model or a relational connection to an adult. Not anymore.

Milestone 3
'Preparing for Adolescence' Topics
▶ Spiritual milestones
▶ Facing the challenges of junior high/ middle school
▶ A look at today's culture
▶ Faith that prevails
▶ Planning the Road Trip Celebration
▶ Milestone 3 resources for families

Milestone 3 Church Event

We offer a 24-hour fourth- and fifth-grade retreat every year. While each year's theme is different, we always highlight one or more of the core competencies and specifically address issues to help children prepare for adolescence. Children whose parents don't think they're ready for the retreat in fourth grade can wait until fifth grade. Some children attend the retreat in both grades. During the time leading up to this retreat, children have been learning the core competencies of identity in Christ, spiritual growth, and spiritual disciplines for practical application in a preteen world not only at home but also in Sunday morning Bible study. The theme of each retreat engages preteens around the core competencies in a kid-friendly and fun way. We have three or four lessons that focus on thanking God for our bodies. We don't address sexual purity. Instead we offer resources to parents of fifth- and sixth-graders and encourage them to take their children on a special getaway to have a conversation about sexual issues.

▶ God Sightings

First 'Date'

Recently my husband asked my daughter to go out on a dinner date—no agenda, just building their relationship and setting a foundation for her future dating relationships. My younger son knew about their plans and asked me to go out with him on a date of our own. He took great pains to look nice and treat me sweetly. It was a precious night with fun conversation. Leaving the restaurant, he held my hand and walked me to the car. He said he wanted to marry someone like me. It was cool to be able to discuss with him the character traits he'd be looking for in a future wife. That night we prayed for the girl who'd be his wife, and he's only 10. —The Loch Family

Milestone 3 Family Celebration

After the retreat, the culmination of Milestone 3 is a family celebration called Road Trip. In the Preparing for Adolescence seminar, parents learn how to plan a road trip to celebrate their children's transition from childhood to adulthood. The purpose of the road trip is to facilitate a fun weekend between father and son or mother and daughter or whatever the family structure allows. The road trip involves connecting with the child relationally around something enjoyable. I know a mom who took her daughter on a weekend shopping trip to the San Antonio River Walk. One father in our church took his son hunting in the hill country, so he'd have a chance to communicate honestly with his boy.

Along the way, parents use the drive time to talk about specific issues, such as physical changes, puberty, emotions, and the importance of making choices that honor God. This is not a "cold turkey" conversation. The conversational aspect of the road trip is effective only if it evolves naturally from months of Faith Talks and discussions leading up to Milestone 3. These conversations are difficult for many parents, but no matter how awkward it feels, children need to know that their parents will lead them relationally as they become teenagers. Currently at Kingsland, we suggest parents use James Dobson's CD series *Preparing for Adolescence.* As an option for the road trip, parents can play excerpts from this CD or other recommended CDs on the way to their destination.

Stories Along the Path

The Father Inside

Your family-focused milestones teaching is invaluable to families, particularly mine. I wanted to share with you my experience with my boys in having the "talk" about life. As you know, I have three boys, ages 14, 11, and 7. My 14-year-old's response was different from the 11-year-old's, and I'm sure I'll be even more surprised by our 7-year-old.

For my trips with each of my older sons, I made arrangements to get an offshore fishing guide in Galveston. We left early Friday afternoon, our vehicle loaded with favorite junk foods, and headed to the hotel. After checking in, we went out to eat wherever my son wanted. We began our dinnertime with prayer and asked God to be honored by what we talk about and my responses to questions. After dinner we went back to the hotel where we prayed, read Scripture related to men, women, and relationships, and talked about life: boys and girls, what's acceptable and what's not, marriage, waiting to have sex and why it matters, and the importance of praying for your future girlfriend and mate.

I'd compiled information from appropriate sources, mostly biblical, and after we reviewed this material, we took time for questions and answers, with the understanding that I'll be available for Q & A until God calls me home. This is when it got difficult, particularly when they asked, "Dad, what did you do?" God is faithful, though, and Laura has committed to pray for our safety and God's presence during this time of teaching and bonding. At the end we prayed and asked God to build into my son the character and purity that God desires. When we were through I made sure my son understood how proud and honored I am to be his dad. Because I learned from a military-style father, I can be harsh at times with the boys, but God is working on me concerning that. After our talk we had a junk food fest and watched a little TV before bed. We got up early the next morning. Breakfast consisted of prayer, finishing off the junk food, and asking if there were any other questions. Then we headed out for our boat trip. Captain John loaded all the gear and gathered everyone around and asked that we pray for safety and success before we go out. Remarkably, I didn't know this about him when I first took my 14-year-old.

I feel an overwhelming obligation to teach, mentor, understand, stand with, pray for, love—father—my boys. Failure to father is scary, although not the end. With the Father inside, the father that I want to be will mature as my boys do. With God's grace, they'll see and remember the Father in me and forget the father I was. —THE HUGHES FAMILY

Milestone 4 ◀

Milestone 4:
Commitment to Purity

"Don't you realize that your body is the temple of the Holy Spirit, who lives in you and was given to you by God? You do not belong to yourself, for God bought you with a high price. So you must honor God with your body" (1 Corinthians 6:19-20).

Church Leader:	Youth pastor or volunteer youth ministry leader
Parent Seminar:	Commitment to Purity
Church Event:	Commitment to Purity Weekend
Family Celebration:	Purity Ring Celebration
Core Competencies:	Biblical purity, healthy relationships, identity in Christ

Milestone 4: What It's All About

Purity for life is a foreign concept in mainstream culture. Without a foundational moral source like the Bible, young people face a chaotic number of relational options. But God has a clear plan for life, relationships, marriage, and sex. In the 1990s the biblical principles behind the True Love Waits campaign brought about a generation of young people committed to remaining sexually pure and saving sex for marriage, as an act of love to God and to their future spouses. We've simply broadened the issue because it's our desire to lead young people to become men and women who live a total lifestyle of purity whether single or married.

Several years ago at our church's summer youth camp, I led a chalk talk for guys based on the book *Every Young Man's Battle* by Stephen Arterburn and Fred Stoeker. I gave the talk twice. To the surprise of the first group—about 100 junior high guys—I asked all the adult sponsors to leave the room for 10 minutes. Then I took a quick, very unprofessional survey, asking the guys to be completely honest with me. "Raise your hand," I said, "if you've looked at pornography on the Internet in the last month." I was devastated to see 90 percent raise their hands. Two hours later I did the same survey with about 100 high school guys. The results were even more dreadful. This time 100 percent of the young men in the room raised their hands. What did I learn? These great Christian kids from middle class suburbia were being slowly devoured from the inside out. Without change, many of them would grow up with a warped sense of sexuality and extreme feelings of guilt. Some of them would drag a crippling sexual addiction into their marriages. To be honest, I cringed as the facade was pulled away.

Is it possible to fight the disconnected, relationally despondent, sexually stimulated Internet culture of America? I think it is. But it means doing much more than simply telling kids to wait until they're married to have sex. Milestone 4 is about equipping parents to lead their sons and daughters to embrace the biblical principle of purity for life.

Milestone 4 Champion

The youth pastor oversees the work of Milestone 4 at our church, but a family pastor, a volunteer youth ministry coordinator, or a church member or parent with training in this area could also fill the role. Whoever takes this on should be someone keenly interested in teaching and motivating young people in grades six through eight and their parents about the issues associated with purity for life. The Milestone Champion ensures that integration is occurring between the youth ministry experience at church and parents' spiritual direction at home. He or she chooses an age-appropriate small group Bible study curriculum that complements the core competencies associated with Milestone 4. This champion equips volunteers to emphasize the core competencies as they come up in small group Bible study. While we don't want parents to talk only about purity for three years, the Milestone Champion helps parents address these principles with Faith Talks, God Sightings, and tools from our resource center. The champion oversees the Parent Seminar and the church event.

Milestone 4 Parent Seminar: Commitment to Purity

Milestone 4 requires the church to equip parents to model purity for life and teach the core competencies of biblical purity, healthy friendships, identity in Christ, and God-honoring sex. We encourage parents to attend the Milestone 4 seminar when their children begin sixth grade. At the seminar parents receive practical tools for helping their kids make a commitment to purity in an impure culture, and they're challenged to model biblical purity. Young people whose parents genuinely love each other, stay pure physically and mentally, and live an authentic Christian faith at home are most likely to make a lifelong commitment to purity.

The seminar offers parents a crash course on the spiritual training of children in this age group. We provide helpful books and other resources for Faith Talks and give parents guidelines for making the most of God Sightings along the way. Parents learn that their job over the next three years is to keep the lines of communication open in regard to purity and relationships. The church comes alongside, echoing parents' voices as they lead and model.

The most powerful moment in our seminar comes when high school seniors speak to parents about the realities of sex within student culture. We choose spiritually mature young people who are willing to talk about their own struggles in middle school and high school related to purity. They spell out what their parents did well and what they did poorly to instill the biblical principles associated with a commitment to purity. They talk about the importance of a parent's example and how detrimental it is when Mom or Dad is hypocritical in this area. These young people explain how being able to talk to parents about sex and pornography provides a huge safety net. And get this—they answer any questions parents want to ask about the pressures of sex in the seniors' personal

Milestone 4
'Commitment to Purity' Topics
▶ Biblical standard for purity
▶ Biblical perspective on sex and intimacy
▶ Identity in Christ
▶ Accountability
▶ Healthy relationships
▶ Leading Faith Talks on purity
▶ Understanding the Commitment to Purity Weekend
▶ Purity ring presentation
▶ Milestone 4 resources for families

lives. In my book, these young people are heroes, dramatically influencing and motivating parents.

Milestone 4 Church Event

In the spring of each year, we offer Commitment to Purity Weekend for eighth-graders and their parents. This culminating event launches young people into a lifestyle of purity with their parents as their guides. On Friday evening the youth ministry brings in a representative from the local pregnancy help center to offer a Bible-based message about sex and to show the consequences of sex outside of covenant marriage. We talk in detail about everything from sexually transmitted diseases to abortion and then contrast the goodness of God's plan for sex with the pain of a false view.

Parents who have led their children spiritually along the path to Milestone 4 are prepared for Commitment to Purity Weekend. The youth ministry and the pregnancy help center only reiterate the principles parents have been teaching for months. Parents participating in Commitment to Purity Weekend as a one-time event without ever leading Faith Talks, capitalizing on God Sightings, and having honest conversations are usually disturbed by this weekend event. They're disturbed because they hear the church addressing issues designed by God to first be addressed at home by parents.

On Saturday the event is focused on helping parents support their children in an effort to live purely. Families discuss ways in which they can stay open and honest with each other throughout the teenage years and overcome the walls that sometimes spring up between parents and teenagers. They look at the scriptural view of sex and God's plan for our spiritual growth. They explore the Bible's role in determining boundaries in all kinds of relationships. Parents and children talk about the characteristics of healthy friendships and the need for parental accountability and mentorship. They explore identity in Christ as the basis for making decisions about who or what we give ourselves to mentally, physically, and spiritually. Finally, we offer young people purity commitment cards and encourage them to take these cards home and talk over their decision with their parents that evening. After a long day of conversation and fun, parents and their children leave having honestly discussed the issues from a biblical perspective. This is imperative. Kids live in a culture bombarding them with lies about personal purity. Families and church can only combat this assault when they work together to tell the next generation the truth.

Commitment to Purity Weekend ends in celebration. During the Sunday morning worship services, eighth-graders choosing to make a lifelong commitment to purity are invited to come to the front of the worship center with their parents. The Milestone Champion spends a few minutes explaining the significance of this event to the congregation. Then he asks each teenager to turn and look at his or her parents and join hands as he reads the commitment they've signed (see below). The congregation witnesses this commitment, while the pastor again highlights the milestone path to everyone attending worship.

During this ceremony I'm usually about one foot away from parents and their children. Parents who have been leading Faith Talks and having intentional conversations leading up to this moment are typically overjoyed and utterly emotional. You can tell they've embraced the struggle of the journey to reach this milestone. The same is true of teenagers who have been following their parents along the path.

The ceremony ends with a pastoral blessing and prayer. After worship young people and their parents adjourn to a more intimate family celebration.

'Commitment to Purity' Vow

Moral Excellence

I recognize that there is an absolute standard of right and wrong. While a majority of my peers will make moral choices based on "what feels right at the time," I will make moral choices based on the standards set forth in God's Word, the Bible.

Purity

I will not date anyone who is not a Christian. I will not engage in any activity that I would feel uncomfortable doing if Jesus were visibly present. Should I find myself in a sexually tempting situation, I will flee immorality. If God leads me to marry, I commit to keep my marriage covenant.

Believing in lifelong purity, I make a commitment to God, my family, my friends, my future spouse, and my future children to a lifetime of purity. This commitment means abstaining from any form of sexual immorality and waiting patiently on God to provide a marriage partner.

Milestone 4 Family Celebration

In preparation for the family celebration, our Milestone Champion sends an email to remind parents about what they learned at the Commitment to Purity parent seminar. We've learned not to assume anything and to model situations for them, so this email includes a script to help parents lead the celebration (see below).

At the culmination of Commitment to Purity Weekend, parents take their son or daughter out to lunch or host a special lunch at home in celebration of the Milestone 4 commitment. At this lunch parents present their child with a ring to be worn at all times as a symbolic expression of his or her commitment to purity. Our hope is that teenagers choosing to make this vow will give the rings to their future spouses as symbols of their purity and commitment.

Milestone 4

Commitment to Purity Family Celebration

Celebrate this significant milestone with a special lunch, either at your child's favorite restaurant or at home with his or her favorite meal. The key is to have a mini-ceremony where you communicate important truths to your child. These truths include…

Live a Life of Purity

▶ Share why you want your child to have a life of purity.
▶ Express how proud you are that your child has made the commitment to stay pure in all areas of life.
▶ Talk about the importance of keeping eyes, heart, and mind pure.

Create Boundaries in Relationships

▶ Explain your views about dating.
▶ Teach the importance of setting boundaries.

Keep Communication Lines Open

▶ Commit to being slow to speak and quick to listen.
▶ Explain that you'll ask questions because you care, not because you're trying to "catch" your child.
▶ Plan a weekly Faith Talk to work through spiritual truths together.
▶ Plan four "special occasion" dinners each year for you and your child.
▶ Ask your child to be open with you…this only happens if there's a good relationship.

Read the Bible

Suggested Scripture reading: 1 Corinthians 6:19-20

Pray

Suggested prayer: God, I pray that you will strengthen my child's desire to live a holy life for you. I pray that my child will seek to honor you with body, mind, and soul. May my child's first and lasting love relationship be with you, Lord. Guide my child's steps and help my child run from temptation. Protect my child's purity.

Present the Ring

Say something like, "This ring is a symbol of the commitment you made in the worship service. Wear it proudly as a sign that you're set apart. Cherish it. And each time you think about the meaning of this ring, say a prayer that God will help you stay pure. This ring is not only a symbol for you but also a symbol for your future spouse. I love you and I'm so proud of you.

Stories Along the Path

Now and Always

We're grateful for the input the church had in equipping us to talk to our son about purity. The seminar's guidance and knowing that other friends and church families were going through this at the same time gave us the emotional support, correct information, and the guts to do it the right way. The seminar also gave parents credibility with our kids because the "experts" were giving good information. When young people spoke out on topics that were difficult and talked about experiences from their own lives, it helped us talk to our children. Our kids could understand that it wasn't just us who felt this way. It helped them listen and really hear what was being said. The church prepared us and partnered with us to teach purity. The Bible, the statistics, the people who have "been there," and the older teenagers all assisted in our desire to teach our child the truth.

When the time came to pick out a purity ring, our son chose a ring with a simple cross in the center. We talked about the significance of the ring as a symbol of his purity commitment. We talked about the price of purity. We talked about the gift that his life choices would be to his future wife and children. We agreed to pray for his bride-to-be—that she would make Christ-centered choices all her life just as he was committing to do now for her. I asked him what he envisioned doing with the ring once he married. His reply was "Give it to my son to make the same choice for his future wife."
—The Waid Family

Milestone 5 ◀

Milestone 5:
Passage to Adulthood

"When I was a child, I spoke and thought and reasoned as a child. But when I grew up, I put away childish things" (1 Corinthians 13:11).

Church Leader:	Youth pastor or volunteer youth ministry leader
Parent Seminar:	Preparing My Child for Adulthood
Family Celebration:	Passage to Adulthood Ceremony
Core Competencies:	Roles of men and women, spiritual gifts and service, basic tenets of the faith

Milestone 5: What It's All About

The growth of a child into adulthood is a significant milestone. In American culture the age of 16 represents an important threshold, but the Passage to Adulthood milestone isn't about superficial freedoms such as keys to a new car or the latest model of cell phone. Instead, Milestone 5 delineates the responsibilities associated with becoming a man or woman of God. It also lays out the Bible's expectation that parents will lead their children to become men and women of God before they leave home. This is Milestone 5, a rite of passage given by parents and practically applied by boys desiring to be men and girls desiring to be women.

During this time the church provides opportunities for teenagers to experience their new sense of responsibility and freedom by learning to serve in meaningful ways. We involve young people headed toward Milestone 5 in everything from our parking lot ministry on Sunday morning to international mission efforts in Uganda. We encourage parents to take the lead and serve alongside them. In our church's context we ask teenagers to join us in our mission to love God, love people, and equip the generations, one home at a time.

Milestone 5 Champion

Our youth pastor is the Milestone Champion for Milestone 5. He oversees the parent seminar and ensures that our church's discipleship process for 9th- and 10th-graders teaches the core competencies. He equips small group leaders, giving them the knowledge base and skill set to effectively teach and model Christlike manhood and womanhood. Most important, he builds relationships with parents, nudging them to raise the expectations in their homes by leading and requiring a transition from childhood to God-honoring adulthood. If you were to have a conversation with our Milestone Champion, he'd say that Milestone 5 requires relational finesse. The best picture any child will ever have of what it means to be a Christlike man or woman is of course Dad and Mom. This gets sticky when parents aren't Christlike.

Milestone 5 Parent Seminar: Preparing My Child for Adulthood

This seminar teaches parents to help children identify their spiritual gifts and exercise them through acts of service in their families and in the church. We help parents use the 9th- and 10th-grade years to embrace truth at home through Faith Talks. Regardless of your church's tradition, Milestone 5 requires parents to help their children intellectually own the basic tenets of the faith. Without this, a child won't live as an adult making decisions according to a biblical worldview.

Milestone 5 also gives parents the opportunity to speak candidly with their teenagers about the Bible's

Milestone 5
'Preparing My Child for Adulthood'
Topics
▶ The Bible's perspective on the roles of men and women
▶ Spiritual training of teenagers: parents' role and the church's role
▶ Passage to Adulthood Ceremony
▶ Milestone 5 resources for families

perspective on the roles of men and women in the context of dating, marriage, friendship, the church, and life in general. Using Faith Talks to discuss the characteristics of manhood and womanhood prepares a young person to live well as an adult and to choose a spouse wisely. We use the parent seminar to teach parents these basics. When parents don't understand the biblical perspective, we take time to teach them so they can lead their children.

▶ God Sightings

Mother-Daughter Alone Time

I'd been feeling that I needed time to talk to my 15-year-old daughter alone. So I woke her on a Saturday morning and told her to pack an overnight bag, not to ask questions, and to have a good attitude. We left the house before noon and didn't return until after church on Sunday. We started out with an activity we're passionate about—scrapbooking and journaling—then headed to a hotel. After unpacking we went to the mall for shopping and a movie, then returned to the hotel for quality time alone (of course, we ate chocolate, too). When I put my daughter's feet in my lap and gave her a pedicure, she opened up and told me so many things. God reminded me (each time I opened my mouth to speak) not to talk but instead to just listen. It was hard to do, but I followed through. Because a lot of her conversation was about friends, I told her I wanted to read her the story from the book of Job. Her favorite childhood book is *The Book of Virtues*, so I found the Job story and read it to her on Sunday morning. It was a perfect mother-daughter weekend. —THE HOWARD FAMILY

Why No Church Event for Milestone 5?

We don't do a church event for Milestone 5 because we want parents to take responsibility for the leadership and celebration of this important transition. Milestone 5 is intended to be an intimate experience between parents, their children, and close friends or spiritual mentors.

Milestone 5 Family Celebration

We help parents learn to host a family celebration called a Passage to Adulthood Ceremony. This event is meant to be a memorable occasion that marks the young person's passage from childhood into manhood or womanhood. Often the gathering includes people who have been instrumental in the child's spiritual development toward Milestone 5. If possible, fathers lead the ceremony for their sons, and mothers lead the ceremony for their daughters. Every family designs the ceremony according to its own style and budget. I've attended ceremonies in backyards, and I've attended ceremonies in the most expensive restaurants in

Houston. All were equally meaningful.

The ceremony consists of several sacred moments in which the parent reminds the young man or woman just what he or she has learned about the Bible's view of manhood or womanhood. Others are invited to offer spoken or written blessings. The celebration usually includes a meal and might also include photos showing the young man or woman's physical progression toward adulthood over the past 16 years. Finally parents give a symbol and a blessing to the child now entering adulthood.

Several years ago I attended a rite of passage ceremony for a young man who impressed me with his biblical foundation for manhood, which was well modeled by his father. We had a wonderful evening together and at the end of the night, inspired by the book *Raising a Modern-Day Knight* by Robert Lewis, the father presented his son with a sword. He explained that the sword was to be passed down from generation to generation, as boys became men in the family. Then asking the son to get down on one knee, and addressing him by name, the father offered this charge:

"May you continue on the path you have already chosen…a path of faith in Jesus Christ, of love for others, and of worship. I pray that God will guide your path… that you will reject passivity, accept responsibility, lead courageously, and expect the greater reward.

I charge you to step forward as a young man of God. To forever encourage and support your brother and all your brothers in Christ. To forever honor, protect, and respect your mother, your sister, and all women.

May God continue to open your heart to the richness of God's glory, the truth of God's Word, the depths of God's love, and the fullness of God's grace. I stand here in the presence of these men, these brothers in Christ, and give praise to our most Holy God for giving you as a son to me…yet greater praise I give God for the knowledge that you are not only my son but also my brother in Christ.

May you live a life filled with purpose, God's purpose for your life. May you stand firm on God's promises, seek God's will for your life, and may God bless you beyond measure.

Take this, my blessing, and stand now and evermore as a man of God. My pride in you overflows, and I love you so very much. Thank you for being more than I could hope for and more than I deserve. And thank you, Lord, for blessing me with my son."

Imagine a culture transformed by a generation of young people who were trained and catapulted into God-honoring adulthood by their parents. This is the essence of Milestone 5, the Passage to Adulthood.

My Favorite Milestone…Shhh!

Don't tell my team, I wouldn't want anyone to think I play favorites, but Passage to Adulthood is my favorite milestone because it pushes back against cultural expectations for teenagers in such a biblical way. Forget the car keys and cell phones…give them swords.

Stories Along the Path

More Precious Than Rubies

When we took part in our first Parent Summit, we attended the seminar for Milestone 5, and from all that I saw and heard that day, the Lord put a desire in my heart to train Jessica and celebrate her Passage to Adulthood on her 16th birthday, which was a year away. Preparation for us meant that we needed to live in God-honoring ways and be very intentional in loving the Lord our God with all our heart and with all our soul and with all our strength. Preparation for Jessica meant that she be growing in her relationship with the Lord, again loving him with all her heart, soul, and strength. While none of us was perfect on our part, the Lord was perfectly faithful and gracious. Proverbs 3 became the passage of Scripture that captured all I wanted to convey to my daughter as she approached adulthood. I wanted to encourage her by showing her how good the Lord had been to her and to charge her to love her Lord and Savior, to cherish God's Word, and to commit herself to God and God's ways. In addition, Proverbs 3 resonated in my heart because of the gift Jessica is to us, the trust God placed in us, and our responsibility and privilege in raising her. Proverbs 3:14-15 speaks of the wisdom of God as "more precious than rubies." This is an apt description of Jessica and became the title of our celebration.

I chose to invite women who'd spoken into my daughter's life and who'd helped me through with God-honoring examples and wise counsel. I gave each woman a passage from Proverbs 3 and asked her to write Jessica a letter of encouragement and exhortation based on her passage. I prayed for these women, that the Lord would lead them to write just what he wanted Jessica to hear.

On the day of the celebration, 10 guests joined us and we read to Jessica from the letters we'd written. The words and wisdom conveyed love, honor, and blessing. We then gathered around Jessica to pray over her with more words of blessing. What a privilege for me to offer this gift to my daughter. I gave Jessica a necklace of crystal rubies as a symbol of her rite of passage. —THE BURNSIDE FAMILY

Milestone 6 ◀

Milestone 6:
High School Graduation

"Then he took the children in his arms and placed his hands on their heads and blessed them" (Mark 10:16).

Church Leader:	Student pastor or volunteer student leader
Parent Seminar:	Preparing My Child to Leave Home
Church Event:	Senior Summit
Family Celebration:	Blessing
Core Competencies:	Defending my faith, God's plan for my life, dating, marriage, life skills

Milestone 6: What It's All About

Parents need to prepare teenagers who are in the last two years of high school for the realities of life away from home. We teach parents how to lead discussions about God's plan for their children to become people of influence for Christ, dating and marriage issues, and life skills such as managing finances. We also train parents on how to defend the Christian faith so they can help get teenagers ready for the non-Christian influences they'll confront at college. Parents learn how the church supports these core competencies by teaching them in the context of small group Bible studies and through influential mentoring relationships.

Milestone 6 Champion

Our youth pastor is the Milestone 6 Champion, but in your church this might be a youth ministry leader or a spiritually mature Christian with experience teaching Scripture. The Milestone Champion's role is to shepherd older teenagers and their parents. We've found that when teenagers are in the later years of high school, parents have a tendency to lessen their involvement. But parents need to stay connected relationally and continue to lead their children spiritually. For many parents this is an awkward time. Parents' feelings of denial associated with their children leaving home and teenagers' busyness often leave little room for continued faith influence. The Milestone Champion works to equip parents to launch their kids into life after high school instead of passively letting them go.

As with the other milestones, the champion continues to urge parents to commit to weekly Faith Talks and to spend time with their children, capitalizing on all the God Sightings possible. This champion coaches parents on how to lead conversations about the core competencies. While it's natural and easy for parents to teach their sons or daughters how to change a tire, manage a checking account, cook breakfast, or wash clothes, it's difficult for parents to teach their children how to defend Christian doctrine. This means parents have to be able to respond to questions such as "Who are we and why are we here?" "If God is so good why is there evil and suffering in the world?" The champion helps strengthen parents' understanding of the basic doctrines of Christianity so they can lead Faith Talks that delve into these questions.

On Sunday mornings we offer high school seniors lessons designed to teach the core competencies associated with Milestone 6. We want them to leave home with the ability to defend their faith and the capability to make practical life decisions from a biblical perspective. We use a Focus on the Family curriculum called The Truth Project, which we also offer on Wednesday evenings for parents. As seniors learn about defending their faith at church, it challenges parents to become equipped as well. How else will they have important conversations with their teenagers about difficult issues?

Milestone 6 Parent Seminar: Preparing My Child to Leave Home

At this seminar we show parents how to maximize their opportunities to influence teenagers during the last two years of high school. We offer resources for teaching core competencies and basic life skills, and parents learn the importance of keeping communication lines open during this crucial phase.

If we surveyed parents and asked them which parent seminar is the most overwhelming, they'd probably identify the seminar for Milestone 6. We have two purposes at this seminar. First, we seek to help parents understand the importance of answering hard questions about faith in the security of their own living rooms before their sons or daughters ever take Philosophy 101 at just about any college. We use this seminar to encourage parents to focus on Scripture in a way that will give their children the capability to defend their Christian beliefs.

The second aspect of the seminar is all about relationship. We teach parents to bless their children in writing before they leave home. We take parents on a little trip down memory lane back to their families of origin with a simple question: Did you receive your parents' blessing? Often this question leads parents to emotional places they weren't prepared to go. It also spurs them toward making sure their children know without a doubt that they have Mom and Dad's blessing. God has hard-wired each of us for blessing, so the absence of parental blessing yields a gaping hole in a child's life that he or she carries forever. We teach parents to offer a written blessing so children can read and re-read what parents really think about them. This matters throughout life. It communicates value and worth from the most important relational connection in a person's life: the family of origin.

Milestone 6
'Preparing My Child to Leave Home'
Topics
▸ Dating, marriage, and money
▸ Helping children discover God's plan for their lives
▸ Defending the faith
▸ Parental blessing
▸ Senior Summit
▸ Milestone 6 resources for families

Formal parental blessing is a noteworthy biblical concept. Consider the sibling rivalry between Jacob and Esau for the blessing of Isaac in Genesis 27. Take a moment to read Jacob's blessing for each of his sons in Genesis 49. There's something mysterious and powerful about the blessing from a parent to a child. We never have to convince parents that this is important. They intuitively know it and embrace the concept.

Milestone 6 Church Event

The purpose of the church event called Senior Summit is to create an opportunity for parents to bless children who'll soon be leaving home. Graduating seniors and their parents gather for a meal and a time of reflection, thanksgiving, and celebration. At the end of the evening, we ask parents to lead their sons and daughters somewhere on the church campus for a private moment. After families have gathered around a table, found a spot in the prayer garden, or simply huddled in a corner of any room in the church, parents read the blessings they've written specifically for their children who are about to graduate from high school.

During this part of the Senior Summit, parents weep with joy and emotion as they offer heartfelt blessings to their babies who have become young adults. Teenagers, even the most hardened, gravitate toward their parents' validation and transparency. This is one of the most sacred moments along the path. One that's filled with tears, hugs, and kisses after children receive these blessings. Excited about the future, young people walk away holding their parents' blessings in their hands. The Milestone 6 celebration ushers in a new chapter of life—away from home and on to the testing ground.

Q&A ▶

What If a Parent Doesn't Write a Blessing?

Our youth ministry staff identifies seniors whose parents won't be writing blessings. We connect these young people with adults in youth ministry leadership who have already established relationships with them. Leaders call parents ahead of time and ask permission to give their blessings. Each leader writes a blessing and reads it to a young person with authenticity and emotion at the Senior Summit. In our minds this is equivalent to a priestly blessing. Though it's not the same as a parental blessing, it's meaningful and important.

Blessing for a Daughter

Nicole, you've found great favor in God's eyes. God has blessed you with true beauty inside and out, good health, and great academic achievements. We're so thankful to God for you and your life in Christ. You're a great daughter, sister, and friend. Your daily presence will be missed greatly, but we know we have to let go of life as we know it and let God's marvelous plans for you unfold. We'll never be apart in spirit and will be united in love always.

We pray that God will incline your heart toward him day and night. May your prayers be near to God. May you feel God's presence and learn to hear God's voice clearly and walk in all God's ways. May God lead you to a new church and bless you with teachers, friends, and activities that will bring God honor and glory.

We don't know what the future holds for you, but we know who holds your future, and as you leave "the nest," we'll be cheering you on as you mount on eagle's wings and soar. —The Mortimer Family

Blessing for a Son

Daniel, live as a free man but don't use your freedom as a cover-up for evil; live as a servant of God. Fear God, which is the beginning of wisdom and knowledge. Realize that Christ is where you'll always find peace. Honor those in authority over you, and know enough about the character of God to recognize the wrong path—then run from it. This is my prayer for you as you enter the next chapter of your life:

"Father, please do not let love and faithfulness ever leave my son; I pray that you, Lord, will bind love and faithfulness around his neck and write them on the tablet of his heart. My God, please help him win favor and a good name in your sight and in the sight of his fellow man. Lord, I pray that his relationship with you will teach him to learn to trust you with all his heart and mind and that he will not lean simply on his own understanding. In recognition of your sovereignty, I pray that you will lead his heart to acknowledge you in all his ways. I pray that you will make his path straight. God, I pray that you'll lead him to be humble and not to be wise in his own eyes, to fear you, and to shun evil. In faith, I pray that you will allow him to prosper according to your riches and mercy."

My firstborn son, remember to be strong and courageous. Do not be terrified; do not be discouraged, for the Lord your God will be with you wherever you go. I love you deeply and will pray for you often. I am here whenever you need a friend; my arms will always welcome you with love and a warm hug. I love you. I am proud of you, son. — The Pulliam family

Milestone 7 ◀

Milestone 7:
Life in Christ

"Yes, I am the vine; you are the branches. Those who remain in me and I in them, will produce much fruit. For apart from me you can do nothing" (John 15:5).

Church Leader:	Adult discipleship pastor, pastor of spiritual formation, senior pastor
Equipping Environments:	Small group Bible study, adult education, and worship
Core Competencies:	Prayer, Scripture, authentic faith, obedient follower, disciple-maker, giving/serving, community

Milestone 7: What It's All About

Every adult has a place at the table of Milestone 7—single or married, kids or no kids, young or old, all of us must abide in Christ and join him in the mission. Churches embracing a strategy linking church and home for the spiritual formation of the next generation can't afford to be apathetic about adult spiritual development. All along the path of milestones, we ask adults to be disciple-makers. Adults who become parents are expected to be the primary faith influencers of their children. Adults from every season of life serve in the ministries relating to children and teenagers. The key to this entire strategy involves developing adults who are also parents, volunteer leaders, and deeply committed Christ-followers.

Milestone 7 Champion

At our church the adult discipleship pastor oversees the Milestone 7 journey. Depending on the size and shape of your church, perhaps you have a minister of education, family pastor, pastor of spiritual formation, director of discipleship, or a volunteer adult ministry coordinator. In any case, the person most connected to the spiritual formation of adults should be the Milestone 7 Champion.

This champion has three primary responsibilities. First of all, this person is responsible for the selection of curriculum. Using a curriculum that effectively teaches the Bible, embraces the seven core competencies of Milestone 7, and provides a level of integration for families is important. FaithWeaver, developed by Group Publishing (group.com/faithweaver), supports the path of milestones and integrates Bible study from the preschool level through senior adulthood, so parents and grandparents have a common platform for intentional Faith Talks with children. It also provides take-home tools to help parents with Faith Talks. The strength of FaithWeaver is total integration. Life Bible Study for adults, developed by Clarity Publishers (lifebiblestudy.com), is also excellent biblically and supports the seven core competencies of Milestone 7. It integrates grade six through senior adulthood when it's aligned with Clarity's Student Life curriculum. Online resources include family devotions and teacher tools.

Second, the Milestone 7 Champion equips volunteer leaders to teach the Bible with effectiveness and model life in Christ. If leaders have children, they help them progress along the path of milestones. Why is this important? If leaders understand the strategy and work it, they're likely to influence others to do the same. Our most effective proponents are volunteer leaders who authentically lead their children and transparently share that journey with their small groups.

Finally, this champion works to equip all the adults in our church to pursue life as people abiding in Christ. When adults are also parents, we equip them to lead their children spiritually. This is reflected in our new members class, small groups, specialized course offerings, and events designed for adults.

Milestone 7 Core Competencies

The core competencies associated with Milestone 7 are the seven characteristic life practices of any follower of Jesus. The first four are all about loving God by abiding in Christ. The remaining three are about loving people as Jesus does. If we can lead adults to genuinely understand and practice the seven core competencies, we'll change the world by helping people experience life in Christ.

▶ Prayer

The simplest approach to following Jesus is to watch what he does and do the same thing. We are, after all, imitators of Christ according to Ephesians 5:1-2. When we study the earthly life of Jesus, we find a man of prayer. He gets up early and heads to solitary places to pray. He prays all night. He prays for others. He prays and fasts for up to 40 days at a time. He lives a lifestyle of prayer. This is how he stays connected with God. Jesus' life was so full of prayer that the original disciples took note, saying, "Lord, teach us to pray." Prayer is access— so why do we neglect it? Too busy or too apathetic, we often push prayer away. Life in Christ makes prayer as natural as breathing or drinking water. We need to show adults how to pray and encourage them to do so. Parents who pray tap into God's wisdom and lead their children spiritually.

▶ Scripture

Followers of Christ learn to study Scripture so they can live Jesus' way. If we insist that parents take on the role of primary faith influencers in the lives of the next generation, teaching parents Scripture and how to study it deepens the well from which they can draw. A working knowledge of Scripture allows parents to recognize and use God Sightings along the path of milestones. A solid grasp of Scripture enables parents to effectively live according to a biblical worldview. This makes them models of life in Christ.

Teaching Scripture to adults is a non-negotiable. "All Scripture is inspired by God and is useful to teach us what is true and to make us realize what is wrong in our lives. It corrects us when we are wrong and teaches us to do what is right. God uses it to prepare and equip his people to do every good work" (2 Timothy 3:16-17). Without the truth of Scripture there's no legacy, no milestones, no foundation for equipping the generations.

▶ Authentic Faith

Authentic faith is different from religion. Religion is safe and predictable. Religion is about certain people singing certain songs inside certain buildings on certain days. Religion seeks to impress and fulfill requirements designed by people. Religion can be faked. In many ways authentic faith is exactly the opposite of religion. Authentic faith requires personal risk-taking. It acts on the small voice of the Holy Spirit and loves God with all the heart, mind, soul, and strength. That means we willingly give God our mental process, our emotion and passion, the work of our hands, and the direction of our feet. Authentic faith bows to the supremacy of Jesus as King, recognizing him as the head of every church and every home, according to Colossians 1:18. Authentic faith gives it all back as an act of worship. Authentic faith is not compartmentalized but all consuming. Authentic faith considers God and other people before self in every moment. Authentic faith loves deeply, clothes the poor, and helps the needy. Authentic faith does the hard things. Authentic faith equips the generations naturally and leaves behind Christlike legacy.

▶ Obedient Follower

The word *follower* often has a negative connotation in our culture. We value leadership. Often we see followers as weaker, less educated, less influential people. Yet the most basic action of Milestone 7 is the act of following obediently. The Bible illustrates life in Christ by describing the relationship between a shepherd and his sheep.

Obedient followers know the Shepherd's voice and respond to his direction. We hear Jesus' voice though Scripture, the Holy Spirit, and the counsel of Christlike people, which directly relates to the core competencies of prayer, Scripture, and community. Think of it. What would it be like to have a church full of obedient followers? What would it be like to have a church full of parents who lead their children to become obedient followers by example? That's equipping the generations.

▶ Disciple-Maker

We point adults to every ministry in our church for the opportunity to disciple others. Perhaps youth ministry or children's ministry will provide this chance; maybe retired adults will help create disciples by serving as small group leaders for young married couples. The point is, everyone who's breathing and embraces the Great Commission as a mandate from Jesus has the opportunity to make disciples in the context of ministry at our church.

When adults are also parents, we teach them that their first priority as disciple-makers is their children. This is where Milestone 7 feeds back into the early milestones along the path. As parents grow and embrace all the core competencies of life in Christ, they're also leading their children spiritually as a natural part of their journey. Parent Summits, Faith Talks, God Sightings, and milestone celebrations become part of what they do as disciple-makers.

▶ Giving/Serving

I wish we could describe this core competency using only one word but we couldn't seem to do it. For us *giving* and *serving*, though two words in English, are really one attitude, one heart, and one action. A Christ-follower gives and serves. Jesus said it this way: "If anyone wants to be first, he must be the very last, and the servant of all" (Mark 9:35, NIV). Not only were these Jesus' words, it was also the model of his earthly life. What if we truly gave and served to the point of making ourselves last so everyone else could be first? What if we were truly servants of all? Adults who embrace this core competency join in Christ's ministry to others. Parents who learn to give and serve raise kids who respect others, love others, and prove it by giving and serving. Husbands and wives who give and serve don't divorce. I doubt that kids who experience giving and serving with their parents will ever forget what it's like to love people like Jesus does.

▶ Community

We were designed for community. The problem is that we're conditioned to be individualistic and self-sufficient. The worldview of the Bible and of Jesus is relational and connected. Biblical church is community. As church leaders we can teach community, we can organize for community, and we can pray for community, but interestingly enough we can't force community. It's the work of the Holy Spirit in the lives of people working out their salvation with fear and trembling. We need each other as we grow in Christ and experience life. On the mountaintops, in the valleys, or along the way, we need to journey together and love each other more and more with each step. Walking the path of milestones in community with others is comforting and compelling. Talking, praying, and strategizing together in the context of biblical community gives parents the courage they need to lead their kids spiritually.

Milestone 7 Equipping Environments

Strategically our process relies on three environments to help adults learn to live life in Christ. First, small groups function to teach adults the Scripture and to foster community on a weekly basis. Second, each semester a series of Wednesday night classes offers adults the opportunity to dig deeper into the specific aspects of life in Christ and focus in on the core competencies of various milestones. Third, our weekly worship services immerse adults in Scripture and highlight milestone celebrations as they naturally occur.

Parents who abide in Christ will raise children who abide in Christ. Adults who mentor kids through the children's or youth ministry will influence the next generation to abide in Christ. This is the way of the Shema.

Scenic ◀
Overlook

Shift Your Paradigm

"All authority in heaven and on earth has been given to me. Therefore go and make disciples of all nations, baptizing them in the name of the Father and of the Son and of the Holy Spirit, and teaching them to obey everything I have commanded you. And surely I am with you always, to the very end of the age" (Matthew 28:18-20, NIV).

Sometimes God gives you a task that you simply must do. That's what the path of milestones has been for me. Even writing this book is an act of obedience out of a compelling sense of call. I've spent serious time during the last few years rethinking everything, and the path of milestones is the resulting paradigm shift. But I don't hold the keys to the perfect church model that will engage families and change the culture—you have to rethink this for your context and culture. Now that you have a basic understanding of the strategy, put it aside and ask God to help you grapple with this question: How would our ministry paradigm need to shift to integrate church and family for the spiritual formation of the next generation? Understand that God's answer will be uniquely designed for your church. As you move toward a decision, here are a few things to consider.

Rethink Mission

Most churches have a mission statement and an articulated vision. The vast majority of church mission statements jump right off the pages of books by Rick Warren, Bill Hybels, or Thom Rainer and Eric Geiger (of *Simple Church* fame). God has used these phenomenal Christian leaders to assist churches in becoming healthier, more effective congregations. I owe much of my understanding about strategic thought and healthy church to these giants. Our very mission statement at Kingsland is similar to the ones found in their books.

Yet we had to seriously rethink our mission statement. Although we had a passion for equipping the generations through the family, our statement read: "Kingsland's quest is to guide you on the journey of loving God, loving people, and discovering life's purpose." One day our senior pastor, Alex Kennedy, and I attended a "learning cluster" for senior pastors led by Will Mancini, founder of the Auxano group and author of the book *Church Unique*. Our cluster bounced around the subject of a clearly defined mission. I remained silent for a while, having been invited by my senior pastor and feeling a little out of place. I think I was the only non-senior pastor in the room. A question burned in my mind, though: *When is it okay to change your mission statement?* I waited and waited and then finally blurted out my question. The group's collaborative answer was that it's okay to change your mission statement when changing it would clarify God's unique, undeniable mission for your church.

So we did.

Our mission statement now reads: "Kingsland's quest is to love God, love people, and equip the generations one home at a time." Strategy always flows from mission and vision. You, too, may need to rethink your mission statement if you desire to create a common path for church and home. Family equipping must be a clearly stated aspect of your mission, vision, and values.

Rethink Strategy Together

After wrestling with integrating the discipleship process of church and home in your context, involve others in the conversation. If you have ministerial staff focused on discipleship at any level in your church, begin to think together. Allow time for this process; it may not go as smoothly as you'd like.

I remember beginning this conversation with our discipleship staff. Our senior pastor had recently released a vision statement for the church that included leading parents to be the primary faith influencers of their children.

That vision gave me a blank canvas to paint on within the framework of our overall mission. Empowered by my senior pastor after months of our own discussions, I approached my team. As their leader—fairly new, fairly young, and fairly inexperienced at the time—I asked them a question: "How can we give discipleship back to the family?" I'll never forget the first response. Our student pastor—who's now one of my best friends and a leading advocate for equipping parents to disciple their children—made this statement: "We can't trust parents to disciple their own kids!"

Clearly this wasn't the response I was looking for—but it summed up the prevailing thought in the room. As we went around the table, everyone spoke from the perspective of his or her ministry training and experience. To their credit, they'd all built dynamic, successful ministries. They'd done exactly what they were trained to do, and they were thinking, *Why fix what isn't broken?* I opened the Bible and read Deuteronomy 6:4-9 and Psalm 78:1-8 and then asked, "What are we going to do with God's view of discipleship?" We went on to converse formally and informally for 18 months before we ever took a step toward implementation. Today that same discipleship staff, now called the generational team, is composed of unified champions bent on a common path linking church and home. This wouldn't be true if we'd neglected to take time to wrestle with the issues together.

Simultaneous with our staff discussions, we involved a group of people who represented a balanced cross-section of our congregation: a married couple without kids, a single mom, a stepfamily couple, a traditional family with two kids, parents of teenagers, and a senior adult couple whose kids are older than I am. All of them were people who walk closely with God and who naturally influence others in our church. For several months we discussed equipping the next generation by equipping parents to lead their children spiritually. This focused experience ensured our success in many ways.

During our discussions we reached agreement on things that have proven true over time. First, this is a slow process. We compiled all our thoughts and moved forward toward design and implementation. The emerging strategy became the path of legacy milestones that now composes the very DNA of our church culture. At the time of this writing, it's been four years since we first began to rethink our process.

Second, we expected opposition—not the "in your face" kind but rather a lack of participation. When the church has been doing all the faith training and you suddenly ask families to share the responsibility, parents may not jump right into the partnership. This too has proven true, but we've made steady progress in equipping more parents, motivating more families, and communicating God's plan for the spiritual formation of the next generation.

About two years after implementing the milestone strategy, a consulting group we hired to illuminate our blind spots made an unannounced visit to our church campus on Sunday morning to test our effectiveness. Posing as first-time guests, they walked our hallways and randomly questioned people. Several weeks later when it came time to hear their report, I felt like a kid going to pick up his report card. What I heard made me cry. It was just one small portion of the report, but it was what mattered most to me. They said the "average Joe" walking down the hallways of our church identified the path of legacy milestones as one of the most important aspects of our ministry. Several people listed all the milestones in order so our visitors in disguise could learn about the common path that the families in our church walk.

Rethink Leadership Responsibilities

Implementing a strategy like the path of milestones changes everything. In established churches the change causes a mindset shift for pastoral staff and others serving in volunteer leadership roles. For example, in our case, prior to developing a common path for church and home, the children's minister was responsible for facilitating a dynamic program to teach kids the truth of God's Word. Now her primary function is to equip parents of children to lead their kids along the path of milestones. Secondarily, she develops Bible study, family Faith Talks, and events in support of the milestones. All those on our generational team experienced a similar, intentional transition.

The best way to implement this shift is to rewrite the job descriptions for leaders, whether paid or unpaid. Being part of the conversation from the beginning will help them understand and adjust to the change in strategy. Rewriting job descriptions takes the strategy to a deeper level. It communicates to each person that his or her ministry isn't an appendage or silo—instead, this is how we do ministry and this is your specific role.

Rethink Programming

Existing programming presents opportunities and obstacles for a strategic partnership between church and family. When a church chooses to embrace this partnership, it confronts the issue of time. If we, as the church, expect the family to serve as the primary faith influencers of children and young people, we must give parents the time necessary to have Faith Talks, celebrate milestones, and make the most of God Sightings.

We must learn to align and simplify. Alignment is lining up all the ministries and associated staff or leadership along the common path and focusing on programs or events that effectively move people along this path. Many of our milestone events, such as Parent Commitment Ceremony, Faith Commitment Ceremony, 4th and 5th Grade Retreat, Commitment to Purity Weekend, and Senior Summit, are existing events that we reformatted and renamed to support our process. These established events created opportunity—without any demand of extra time or resources.

We then "simplified" any existing programs that don't help parents and children walk the path, which is a nice way of saying, "cut." Simplification is required because families need time to lead their children spiritually, and the church needs to free up time for a few new equipping events that support the path. To align and simplify is very similar to constantly pulling weeds out of a beautiful landscape. It takes time. They keep growing back. Some weeds are harder to pull than others. Sometimes timing is crucial. Every once in a while you'll find people who really love the weed you're trying to pull. My advice: Convince them to help you pull it.

Give Back the Sabbath

Last spring I was at the Hoan Kibbutz on the shore of the Sea of Galilee when the Sabbath began and families gathered to eat, rest, and celebrate. The next afternoon families lounged around the lake. I watched as young children called out, "Abba!" and ran into their daddies' arms. Some families picnicked; others swam or strolled and talked. In the Hebrew mind, the Sabbath is about three important priorities: God, family, and rest.

As you align and simplify, consider giving back the Sabbath to families and leaders. In the past 14 years I've served in three churches. In the first two churches, we hosted full-blown programming for children, teenagers, and adults from 4:30 on Sunday afternoon until 8:00 in the evening. Who showed up? The core families in the church—mostly because they felt an obligation to be there out of duty or guilt.

Before you judge me a heretic for demeaning Sunday night church services, realize that we've given the Sabbath back to families for a reason. When my family comes home from Sunday worship service, we have lunch. Sometimes we walk to the park. Or I take all three girls somewhere and let my wife rest. The point is we're together and we relax. On Sundays we have our Faith Talk. Often it's in our living room or at the park or in the local Starbucks. We use the time to be together as a family and train our kids spiritually. Giving the Sabbath back affords every parent in our church this opportunity.

Truth be told, we have one remaining program on Sunday evening. A remnant if you will. It's a good program that supports the path but consistently eats into the Sabbath for some families. We'll get there. What have we moved from Sunday night? Worship, Kids Choir, AWANA, deacons' meeting, adult discipleship classes, and every other committee meeting, training session, and small group imaginable. The senior pastor and I constantly contend with requests for Sunday meetings or programs. Sometimes the sheep don't know they need to rest and be with family, so you have to lead them. Give back the Sabbath. Train parents to use Sunday for intentional Faith Talks.

Rethink Equipping Opportunities

The milestones path forces a church to equip adults effectively. In one sense our student pastor was right when he expressed dismay at the idea of partnering with parents. At first we couldn't have trusted all our adults to lead their children spiritually because we'd neglected to equip them for the task. We needed to rethink our equipping opportunities for adults to include offering parents the chance to acquire practical parenting skills, biblical depth for effective faith transformation, and stellar resources in support of each milestone along the path. Three strategic efforts emerged from our time spent rethinking.

▶ Parent Summit Conferences

Parents attend these biannual conferences on multiple occasions as their children enter various spiritual and developmental stages. Every Parent Summit offers all the parent seminars associated with the milestones, including two seminars considered prerequisites. Seminar one is Understanding the Path of Milestones, which describes the path and the beautiful partnership between church and family. Seminar two is How to Lead Intentional Faith Talks, because Faith Talks are the formal platform parents use with their children.

Each Parent Summit conference is unique. Keynote speakers bring biblical perspective, current trends, and expertise associated with their personal ministries, backgrounds, and experiences. Seminars such as What Every Child Needs Parents to Know About Sex, Extreme Grandparenting, and Parenting Prodigals give parents help related to pressing needs. Sometimes administering "first-aid" along the way makes it possible for parents to embrace the path and commit to leading their children toward spiritual maturity.

▶ Resource Center

In 1990, after I'd mowed hundreds of yards, my dad and I split the cost of the first vehicle I ever owned: a red 1984 Nissan King Cab pickup. She had a camper top on the back and flip-down seats in the extended cab. I really thought I was "the man." Part of the deal, of course, involved my taking responsibility for the care of this little truck. Because every tank of gas and every oil change meant mowing another yard, I decided to do the routine maintenance myself. Changing the oil seemed like a fairly easy procedure. I crawled under the truck and drained the oil out of the pan. No big deal. Then I began searching for the oil filter from the top. I opened the hood and looked for several minutes. I spotted the filter in a difficult location. I could get my hand on it, but twisting off the filter was another problem entirely. Knuckles bleeding and sweating profusely, I tried and tried to no avail. I think my dad must have been watching from the window. Like a phantom he emerged from the garage with a tool he called a filter wrench. In two minutes he had the filter in hand. I learned a lesson that day: Having the proper tool for the job makes a difficult situation manageable.

Providing parents with good tools for the task of influencing their children spiritually is a key strategic component of our equipping strategy. Most parents don't even begin to know where to look for the proper tools and resources for the path. We save them time and energy by recommending resources associated with each milestone. (Our list is available at legacymilestones.com.)

Our resource center began as a simple list of books, articles, Web resources, and family devotional guides organized by milestones. We included resources related to developmental stages and to teaching the core competencies. Creating a list of recommended resources for parents is a strategic step all churches can take. Anything from a paper list in a high-visibility location in your church to a PDF document on your church website will suffice. Parents will love you for conducting a "resource review" for them.

A more effective method for supplying parents with excellent resources involves putting tools into their hands the moment they sense a need. For example, we found that offering books and other resources for purchase at the Parent Summit conference gave motivated parents the opportunity to acquire tools we discuss in the parent seminars for each milestone. Having the resources on hand at the event ensures that a higher percentage of parents will invest in resources to lead their children spiritually. So what was once a list became a portable resource center that we set up at the Parent Summit conference and stored in a closet throughout the year. Then slowly, in between Parent Summits, parents began buying books out of the closet. The increasing demand for resources eventually led us to organize a more permanent effort. Now parents can visit the Legacy Resource Center on our campus and select from an array of resources organized by milestone and offered at discount prices. Every Wednesday and Sunday, I observe parents, with coffee in hand, discussing resources. An added bonus is the resource center's visible representation of the strategy, reminding the people of our church to walk the path of legacy milestones.

▶ Equipping Environments

In many churches the most successful equipping environments for adults are weekend worship services and small groups. Maximizing teaching segments within the worship service to motivate and equip allows the greatest number of adults to connect with the strategic integration of church and home. This doesn't mean that every worship service and every sermon becomes about the path of milestones. However, when the Scripture naturally discusses the issues of parenting, family, or spiritual formation, we maximize the moment to equip adults to train their children spiritually. The Bible often provides natural connections to the path of milestones because the strategy flows from the pages of Scripture. If you're a preacher of the Word, preach all of it. Preach it with passion and with integrity.

Worship also provides a wonderful opportunity to give parents a Faith Talk tool. Parents struggle to lead family devotions. Whatever the church can do to help them is important. Each week our pastor writes a short devotion called Table Talk, which we insert into the worship guide. Our pastor also draws attention to this at the end of each service. The idea is simple—the Table Talk flows from the sermon content. Table Talk gives parents an easy way to start conducting weekly Faith Talks based on the key Scripture passage highlighted in that week's worship service. This entry-level opportunity gives everyone the ability to develop the practice of Faith Talks.

Small group environments offer valuable opportunities to equip parents as the primary faith influencers. The process requires every leader to completely understand the strategy and to practice it if they're parents. Understanding the path affords teachers the capacity to capitalize on sections of Scripture addressing parental motivation, biblical core competencies, milestones, and practical examples for use in Faith Talks. The goal is to develop leaders who involve adults in an ongoing conversation, encouraging and equipping parents to walk the path with their children.

At Kingsland we're working to get better at this component of equipping adults. It's almost impossible to over-communicate the strategy with leaders. We work hard to make milestones a part of every leader development opportunity. We use email, the Internet, church publications, even our facility to communicate the strategy. Recently our adult discipleship pastor began adding "milestone moments" to the help sheet he provides to leaders and teachers each week. The idea is to condition teachers to use examples from their personal Faith Talks, their God Sightings along the path, or their milestone celebrations as living illustrations of Scripture. Again, never forced, these moments consistently engage small group participants in the path of milestones. I dream of a day when all our volunteer leaders naturally capitalize on Bible passages that highlight the path, tell stories from their family devotions, and point to resources that are effective in helping parents lead spiritually.

The Payoff

How does making an effort to rethink and align church and family along a common path for spiritual formation yield dividends? This is not penny stock or a gamble. There's no chance for a huge, immediate payoff. Instead, think of this as a long-term investment, maturing with each year that passes. Several benefits to the church and family will emerge in the first few years of implementation.

▶ A Return to God's Original Plan

Perhaps the most significant benefit is the shift of the church toward a biblical plan that expects family to be the leading influencer in a child's spiritual formation. This biblical paradigm shift finds blessing from God when it translates into practice. Aligning the church with God's plans for the next generation deepens the ability of the church to be salt and light. God paves the way and God's hand is completely recognizable in the process.

▶ A Path to Walk On

I regularly receive emails or engage in conversations with the people in my church that go something like this: "Thank you for giving me a path to walk on as a parent. As a Christian I knew I was supposed to lead my children spiritually. I just had no idea what to do. Now I'm encouraged to take one day at a time, one step at a time, and I know where I'm going." Parents find hope in understanding a way to lead their children spiritually. This is an early payoff that will lead to great rewards in the years ahead.

▶ Support From Senior Adults

Senior adults are among the greatest supporters of the milestones path. More than once I've listened to a tearful senior adult who wishes there had been something like the milestones path to help when he or she was raising children. Now as grandparents, senior adults see the tremendous value of a partnership between church and home. They rally around the milestone project. I often make resource suggestions to grandparents who want to gently nudge their adult children to lead their grandchildren spiritually. The elder generation wisely understands the value of spiritual legacy.

▶ Community Interest

Parents from all cultures, backgrounds, and traditions are interested in the spiritual growth of their children. We've experienced a significant amount of community interest around our Parent Summit events. Often a member of Kingsland will quietly share a prayer request for a friend from another faith background who's registered for Parent Summit. Why do they register? They need help parenting their kids. Our church is becoming known in the community as a church that's helping parents and making a difference in the next generation.

▶ Healthy Conviction

Conviction is the work of the Holy Spirit in Christ-followers' lives, which leads us back into a right relationship with God. The path of milestones consistently challenges parents to "step it up" as the primary faith influencers of their children. Sometimes this means a major lifestyle adjustment—even a career change. More commonly, parents find the Spirit convicting them to be intentional about discipleship in the home. We provide parents with a clear method and all the support we know how to offer, helping them live out their commitment.

▶ Impact on the Next Generation

After implementation of the milestone strategy, you will begin to hear stories that add to the fire of your passion to equip the next generation one home at a time. You will observe parents committing to train their babies spiritually with confidence, knowing they have a clear plan to disciple their children. You will witness public commitment of faith by children and teenagers whose parents actually played a role in their spiritual development. You will hear about children and their parents serving on mission trips together around the world. You will attend Passage to Adulthood ceremonies as parents pass the mantle on to the next generation. You will read blessings written by parents to their children and see parents and children weep as they're reunited relationally. My prayer is to look back several years from now and see a growing population of young adult Christians living life biblically.

▶ Shifting Momentum

Certainly my church is a microcosm within a potentially much larger movement. Yet at the same time, within this microcosm a growing number of Christian parents are making the commitment to lead their children spiritually. Imagine the momentum shift if parents from every Christian church in the country embraced this God-given responsibility. From church to church and family to family, we will become a small part of the story of God's love for the generations yet to come.

Make Your Home
the Model

"He must manage his own family well, having children who respect and obey him. For if a man cannot manage his own household, how can he take care of God's church?" (1 Timothy 3:4-5).

Let's pretend for a moment that you and I are having a very private conversation. This is a safe conversation. Setting up the appointment was a difficult experience for you. *I'm a pastor, for goodness' sake,* you thought to yourself as you made the call to schedule the date and time. You comprehend the importance of the meeting, though you're uncomfortable about its necessity. As a church leader launching a new strategy integrating church and home, you struggle with the model of your own family life. For years your mode of operation included masking your personal life and teaching your family to wear a church persona for the sake of your ministry. You're struggling with the uneasy reality that your plan for the spiritual development of your own children is lacking—at best. The spiritual battle you now face requires authentic faith lived most passionately in the place you feel most pathetic and least passionate as a leader: home. How can you ever make your home the model?

Unfortunately, many of us as pastors and church leaders struggle most where it matters most. It's generally impossible to fake Christianity with the people who call us husband or wife, Mom or Dad. At home, all walls are down. There's no act, no special title or office of importance. Family is the relational context in which we offer the most authentic view of our faith, whether positively or negatively.

Sadly, we all hear the "pastor's kids" jokes. We know pastors who place the abundance of their efforts and energy into the church, neglecting the most important people in their lives. Secretly worried that we too prioritize our time in a way that puts church before family, we wonder what kind of light will shine on our efforts to lead our own children spiritually. What will the "special microscope" issued to people when they join our churches reveal about our ability and efforts to disciple our own children? It's a fair question. If you're a pastor or ministry leader and you have children, planning for their spiritual development is not only a biblical requirement, it's also the primary experiential model for a strategy linking church and home to equip the generations. You'll teach, lead, and equip often from your own experience. Better make sure you have it.

Become Like Standing Stones

In the Middle East today as you travel on foot, you'll occasionally find unnaturally placed large rocks called "standing stones." This ancient practice of setting stones created memorials to a magnificent work of God. The stones are a constant reminder of God's presence, provision, and power. Sometimes the stones protrude 10 feet into the air. They're an awe-inspiring sight and a testimony to the work of God in the lives of people. Weary travelers become curious and wonder, "What did God do in this place?"

Throughout Scripture God uses people as standing stones just as people used magnificent rocks. God sets these people in obvious places so when others pass by they see a testimony of God's presence, provision, and power. In our culture God still reminds us by using people as standing stones set in obvious places, people whose lives point others to God. Think about it for a moment. Where does this matter most? In the home—where God sets parents.

Two kinds of Christian parents exist in the world today: those parents who live spiritually as standing stones and those who live as stumbling blocks. Standing stones walk as Jesus did. Christian parents living as standing stones aren't perfect but they're pursuing an authentic relationship with Jesus. You can identify parents like these by their passion for obedience. In the gusty cultural winds of 21st century America, our children need those to whom they can anchor their lives. God designed parents as the perfect rocks in which our children find stability and shelter.

Establish a Bema Stone

First-century synagogues were places of worship, spiritual instruction, and formal education. If you enter a synagogue from the time of Christ, you'll find a stone, called a bema stone, setting on the floor in a prominent location. From the bema the Torah was read so the people could hear the words of the Lord, celebrate them, and adjust their lives to the words. In our churches today we call this spot the pulpit, but the pulpit you speak from at church is inadequate for leading your own children in the faith. We need to establish a bema in our homes so our families can hear the words of God, celebrate them, and adjust life accordingly. The bema stone of Christian parenting is the intentional Faith Talk. It's the place of permanence in your home where the family comes together to hear the truth, celebrate it, and adjust life to it.

Faith Talks are a time set aside each week to focus on biblical truth in an age-appropriate, relational way. Faith Talks don't have to be difficult—or even formal. We once walked to the park at four o'clock in the afternoon in the middle of the summer in Houston. After about three blocks my kids were red-faced and sweating. Intentionally, we stopped under a large live oak near the bayou. I asked my kids to step in and out of the shade and tell me the difference. Of course they commented on the cool shade provided by the tree that protected them from the sun. I reminded them of Isaiah 25:4 as it describes God. *"But you are a tower of refuge to the poor, O Lord, a tower of refuge to the needy in distress. You are a refuge from the storm and a shelter from the heat."* We also talked about Psalm 121:5, *"The Lord himself watches over you! The Lord stands beside you as your protective shade."* When circumstances are difficult and we need protection, we turn to God, who is our cool, refreshing, protecting shade in the middle of the desert called life. God is our shade. We prayed and walked the rest of the way to the park and enjoyed the afternoon.

My goal for our family Faith Talks is to create a relational, fun experience that provides a platform—a bema stone of sorts—from which we can read the words of God as a family, celebrate them, and adjust our lives accordingly. We started this discipline with our children when they were very young. Now it's a way of life at our house. I suspect we'll face drama and attitude on occasion as we teach our girls truth, but impressing the commands of God on our children isn't contingent on their choices, attitudes, or opinions. Establish your bema stone. Make Faith Talks an intentional time to lead your children spiritually.

Overcome Stumbling Blocks

Believe me, I understand what you're thinking right now: *This is all great in theory, but how will it play out in my living room?* I entertained these same thoughts in the beginning. Here's how to overcome these common mental stumbling blocks.

We don't have enough time to prepare and consistently lead a weekly Faith Talk. Most church leaders with families are busy. Between homework, the kids' extra-curricular activities, and all our church responsibilities, little time is left over for anything else, but it's time to slow down and prioritize. Again we have a biblical mandate to lead our children in the faith. Something has to go to make time for at least a weekly Faith Talk.

I'm not adequately equipped to lead a Faith Talk. Ironically, in spite of all our seminary training and ministry experience, it's common to feel awkward about leading Faith Talks. Seminary in no way prepared me to lead my children spiritually. Leading a talk that connects with an 8-year-old or a 15-year-old may be outside your comfort zone, but this isn't an excuse. Just like every other parent in your church, you must equip yourself. You can find dozens of good resources out there to help you lead Faith Talks. Your strategy should be as simple as this: Read and apply.

My kids are high school students and starting this now will be too difficult. You're in for a struggle initially, but, nonetheless, even if you're starting late you need to shoulder the responsibility to lead your children. Slow your teenagers down enough to spend time together talking about God's Word as it relates to life. Relate it to their lives. Get into their world. Study their culture. Discover their spiritual gifts and understand their emotional needs. Get to know their friends, learn what happens in their classrooms, research their Internet patterns, and listen to them. Use this information to create practical

Faith Talks that teach biblical core competencies. You may encounter some resistance—but what's a little resistance in comparison to knowing you did everything you could to lead your child to embrace relationship with Jesus?

I don't have the energy to do this. If you're like me, by the time Sunday afternoon rolls around, you're beat. *After all, the Sabbath is for rest,* I tell myself. Sometimes I'm tempted to forgo our Faith Talk on Sunday evening because of the mental effort it will take to pull it off. The stumbling block of fatigue rears its ugly head, and I think to myself, *We can do this tomorrow.* Typically, if I take that step backward, our Faith Talk gets skipped altogether that week. I've found this to be the common experience among other ministry leaders committed to Faith Talks. But I've arrived at a place of conviction in my life where the following statement sums it up for me—and it's not an indictment of you personally: It is weak, apathetic, passive, and passionless to lay aside intentional faith training because we're tired. We must be more passionate about the spiritual formation of our own children than we are about the spiritual formation of those who attend our churches. We'd never say, "I'm not going to fulfill my ministry responsibilities today because I'm too tired." Reject passivity, push away apathy, and be courageous. Commit to a consistent time each week for Faith Talks and guard it as closely as you guard your church attendance on Sunday morning.

Walk the Path With Your Family

The path of milestones is designed for families. Parents intentionally lead their children to grow in the faith. Pastors and church leaders equip parents to do this by providing resources and experiences that enhance the journey. As a parent, walk the path with your family. Celebrate milestones. Intentionally teach biblical core competencies through Faith Talks and God Sightings. Pour your heart into leading your child or teenager along the path. Attend events at your church designed to enhance your ability to lead your children spiritually or to highlight the truth you've been teaching them at home. As a parent you walk the path for the sake of your own children. As a pastor or church leader you walk the path as a model for all the other parents struggling to do the same. In this way you authentically equip the generations one home at a time, beginning with your own.

Tell the Stories of Your Journey

You and I need to tell our people stories from our family lives. We need to let people in so they can see our successes and failures. Without embarrassing or exposing our children, we need to share our mistakes as parents. We need to speak to our successes. People need to hear that their pastors and ministers lead from a place of authenticity and experience. This strategy isn't a philosophy or a theory but a way of life. Telling your story connects people to a lifestyle, not just a strategy.

A Final Word: Listen

Shhh…listen. Do you hear the footsteps? These are the footsteps of the generations following us as we walk a common path for the spiritual formation of the next generation. These are the footsteps of thousands of church leaders walking the path and effectively equipping the generations one home at a time by leading parents to be the primary faith influencers. This is the sound of parents equipped and motivated to lead their children along the path of milestones. If you listen closely you'll hear the sound of cultural redesign. In every home and with every milestone, we take one step closer to actually living out the Shema in the 21st century. This is the sound of spiritual reformation in our world. Soon the sound of footsteps walking the path will be much stronger—strong enough to change the direction of our culture. Will you join us?

Road Service ◀

FAQs and Helpful Tools

Remember—the milestones strategy is a one-step-at-a-time, one-home-at-a-time project. You don't have to be up and running tomorrow. A strategic discipleship plan integrating church and home manifests its success over time. Patience, strong resolve, and a deep sense of calling must characterize those committed to this undertaking.

Here are the questions I'm asked most often by church leaders and parents.

How do you measure the effectiveness of the milestones strategy?

For us, measuring success means capturing parents' stories as they walk their children toward the next milestone, recognize God Sightings in their daily lives, and seize opportunities to teach their children. Success is being invited to watch as families host milestone celebrations; it's reading emails and notes from parents empowered to lead their children spiritually. We celebrate the little things and trust God for the generations.

We know that average attendance at our Parent Summits has grown from 100 to more than 500. We also measure attendance at each of the parent seminars supporting a milestone, the number of books purchased from the resource center, and the hits on our websites that indicate interest. We've started conducting surveys four times a year in our worship services to help our staff discern how many adults are walking the path to some degree. More than 600 adults with children living at home responded to our most recent survey. When asked if they celebrate Legacy Milestones as they lead their families, more than 70 percent said yes. More than 35 percent said they have intentional Faith Talks once a week with their families. And almost 93 percent said they use God Sightings as teaching opportunities. This is unscientific data but it gives us a reasonable indication. (You'll find our survey template on page 136.)

How do parents discover where their children are along the path so they can lead them to the next milestone?

At each Parent Summit conference we help parents map their course to discover what milestones their kids are headed to next. Parents quickly learn the specific parent seminars they'll need to attend. We use a simple tool called Chart Your Course that includes a step-by-step checklist to help parents plug into the milestones strategy or find help if they get lost along the way (see page 137). In five minutes, parents can discern their current location and chart a course for leading their children spiritually.

Do families have to start at the beginning?

Absolutely not—churches will always have new families coming in who never thought of leading their kids spiritually or imagined finding a church that would help them with this process. We're finding as the years go by that more and more people start at the beginning, but we'll always demonstrate how to enter the path from the perspective of each family's current life season. It's quite possible that families entering the path will have kids who are at Milestone 2 and Milestone 5 or any other combination of milestones. Be flexible and help them all walk the path.

What about kids whose parents don't lead them along the path of milestones?

Not all parents will lead their children spiritually. If the major thrust of your discipleship ministry puts parents in the driver's seat, what happens to children whose parents don't invest in them spiritually? The simple answer is they'll continue to experience church and discipleship just as they would have if we'd never developed a strategy integrating church and home. Our volunteer leaders in the context of children's ministry and youth ministry will walk them along the path of milestones. This isn't the best-case scenario, but it's no worse than the status quo in most churches today. We can't decide to avoid developing strategies integrating church and home because some parents won't participate. Instead we build the strategy and work hard to make the church side of it as effective as possible for kids whose parents will never lead them spiritually. Never underestimate the God factor. God takes kids from apathetic, traumatic, and even tragic homes and turns their spiritual lives into a triumph. When a child needs primary faith influencers and Mom and Dad shirk their responsibility, the church will lead the way.

How can parents lead quality Faith Talks with children of multiple ages?

It's certainly a challenge to lead intentional Faith Talks in a family with kids at different age levels, but it's a challenge most parents will face. Our kids' current ages are 9, 6, and 18 months. The 9-year-old is quickly moving toward Milestone 3, the 6-year-old is on her way to Milestone 2, and the 18-month-old has checked off the Milestone 1 box. Our strategy is to lead Faith Talks in ways that interest all of them. We work hard to keep it interactive, with sensitivity to each child's level of spiritual development. For instance, we don't address preparing-for-adolescence topics during our regular Faith Talks. Instead we lead Faith Talks that everyone can learn from and then spend individual time to help each one with her upcoming milestone. The best answer is that parents lead quality Faith Talks by knowing each child's needs and using common sense. It takes individual time with children to address certain issues.

Think of Faith Talks as a vehicle. Maybe our 9-year-old is going to a soccer game, our 6-year-old is headed to a birthday party, and our 18-month-old is just along for the ride. Though they're all headed different places today, there's value in getting everyone into the family vehicle to reach each of our respective destinations. There's also value in gathering the entire family into the vehicle of a Faith Talk to get where we're going. Though the short-term destinations may be different, in the long term we'll end up in the same place together.

How do you keep the milestones strategy in front of your people?

We make a constant effort to keep the milestones strategy in the minds and hearts of the people of our church. We do this in a number of ways. All prospective new members at Kingsland take a class called Next Step. In Next Step we do a mini-milestones seminar to explain our vision and strategy for equipping the generations one home at a time, acknowledging parents as the primary faith influencers. When people join the community of Kingsland, they understand the integration of church and family and the expectation to walk the path of milestones. This is a very important aspect of developing momentum in a growing body of believers.

We also use one primary graphic illustration in publications, promotional pieces, and throughout the church to remind people of the responsibility and action of walking the path. Part of keeping the idea in front of people is to do it visually and subliminally. They catch glimpses of the strategy as they walk down the hall at church, surf our website, get coffee in the resource center, or check their email. In a quiet way we're always whispering, "Remember, seven milestones and a path to walk."

As described earlier, we use our resource center as a way to equip parents but also as a method of keeping the process in front of people every Wednesday and Sunday. It's beautiful to watch people go in for coffee and come out having read, asked questions, or purchased supplies to help them lead their children spiritually. (You can a find a copy of our most up-to-date resource list at legacymilestones.com. Our list is constantly changing as we add new books and develop new tools.)

Our pastor does a great job of keeping the vision in front of the church by providing a weekly Table Talk devotion based on his sermon. We put this into the worship guide and consider it a highly effective way to constantly remind our people to take this small step each week.

We also use the Parent Summit conference twice a year and regular interactive conversation points in the form of podcasts and blogs that invite parent comments. You can find these conversation points at legacymilestones.com and legacyblog.org.

Finally, we keep the milestones strategy in front of our adults with Take-Home Sunday four times a year. On these Sundays every adult small group discusses a milestones topic. On pages 133-135, you'll find an adapted Take-Home Sunday lesson by Josh Allen, adult discipleship pastor at Kingsland.

Take-Home Sunday
When You Walk by the Way
Key passage: Deuteronomy 6:6-7

▶ Opening

My Story: Relate your own story to the class about the birth of your child. For example: I'll never forget the first time I laid eyes on her. She was born weighing 6¾ pounds, and just gazing at her little bald head and big blue eyes melted my heart. For her, life was new and she was a sponge soaking it all in. For me, her innocence drove me to prayer. My actions, responses, successes, failures, hugs, kisses, and words would shape her. Her world would soon be filled with the things I allowed to enter her precious mind. The weight of that responsibility sent me to my knees and the Bible with new clarity. God had chosen to trust my wife and me with this little life.

Say: **Turn to a partner and discuss these questions:**
• **How did it make you feel when the responsibility to raise your little one hit you?**
• **When the day arrives that your child leaves your home, who do you want your child to be spiritually?**

▶ Exploring Scripture

Say: **Deuteronomy 6 holds far more than inspirational verses about developing our children. It contains a strategy of sorts for tackling what will most likely be the greatest challenge of parenting. Let's take a look at that.** Form groups of four. Have parents open their Bibles to Deuteronomy 6:4-7. Have each group read the Scripture and answer these questions.

Say: **According to this Scripture…**
• **What's God's responsibility to your children?**
• **What's your responsibility to your children?**
Allow five minutes.

Bring everyone back together and ask for reports on what they talked about.

Then say: **In Deuteronomy 6:5 we see that loving God with all our hearts, mind, and strength can't be done apart from a relationship with God. Rules, regulations, religious practices, and even morality don't constitute a relationship with God. It would be as if you and your spouse lived according to the rules of morality in marriage but never spoke or connected. You simply lived with one another according to the "rules"—without the relationship.**

In Deuteronomy 6:6 two specific points rise to the surface that play a large role in how we read and apply this passage. Verse 6 indicates that parents need to be walking with God before they guide their children to do the same. This doesn't imply perfection or working knowledge of all Scripture. This passage implies that God is leading us in our daily lives.

Point 1: As parents, we model a relationship with God, or we model adherence to religious rules. We either paint a beautiful image of God in our children's hearts or we paint a distorted view of a judgmental cosmic rule enforcer. Leading our children to walk with God begins naturally from our own walk with God.

Point 2: A relationship leads to obedience. Deuteronomy 6:6 takes the next step of relationship with God, which is obedience to follow out of love—"Commit yourselves wholeheartedly." In our walk with God, relationship fuels obedience. The message of obedience is simple: Are you following God in a loving relationship?

In Deuteronomy 6:7 we see what "doing life" looks like. Let's dig deeper into this Scripture.

Divide the entire class into four sections; have people stay in their groups of four. Assign the first section: "when you sit at home"; the second section: "when you walk along the road"; the third section: "when you lie down"; and the fourth section "when you get up."

Say: Today we're going to discuss one key aspect of instilling truth into the lives of our children, no matter their ages. God is constantly at work in and around us. We have a unique responsibility to guide our children to recognize this. God Sightings are the moments when our children express an interest or awareness that provide an opportunity for us to talk about God. God Sightings are also when we spot God at work in our lives.

Think about your assigned area. What's one way you've had a God Sighting with your child in that area? Maybe there's a time that you've been sitting around watching TV and a show sparked a talk about God with your child. Or maybe right before bed, your child asked a question about God. Maybe you review the day together and look for at least one God Sighting each day. Share that in your groups. If you don't have one you've done, think of something you *could* do in that area.

Allow time. Then bring groups back together and have each group tell a few God Sightings.

Say: Those are great ideas. God Sightings are around us all the time. "Walking along the way" requires us to spend time with our children so we spot those God Sightings. If we don't see our children because of schedules, conflicts, and busyness, we'll never be able to capitalize on the teachable moments God is revealing. Parenting takes time. A relationship of freedom and authentic love takes time.

Make the time you have with your kids meaningful. Turn off the TV, PlayStation, or other distractions and play together. Rearrange priorities to honor the most important relationship any of us has—our family.

▶ Prayer
Say: It may seem obvious, but take prayer beyond mealtimes. Remember the four areas we talked about for God Sightings from Deuteronomy 6:7. Pray at home, in the car, at bedtime, in the morning…all the time!

Let's pray now.

God, we pray for sensitivity. Please open our hearts to see where you're at work in our children.

We pray for wisdom. Give us insight and discernment to capitalize on teachable moments.

We pray for courage. Give us strength and confidence to engage in spiritual conversations that may seem uncomfortable.

We pray for patience. Help us be quick to listen and slow to speak.

Help us foster an open dialogue and a loving connection.

Help us make our homes the safest place for our children to ask life's hard questions.

In Jesus' name. Amen.

▶ Wrap-Up

Pass out blue stress balls, shaped like water drops and labeled "God Sightings."

Say: **If you imagine your child's life as a pool of water, God Sightings are each just one drop. But when you capitalize on these moments, the ripple effect will change the entire pool of water. Place this drop where it will be a daily reminder to look for God Sightings in your life, your child's life, and the life of your family. In two weeks, we're going to take time to discuss the God Sightings that we've seen in our families' lives.**

Survey:
Parents With Kids Living at Home

▶ **Mom or Dad** *(please circle)*

▶ **Age:** 20s, 30s, 40s, 50s *(please circle)*

▶ **Age of children** *(please circle)*

Birth to age 5

1st grade to 6th grade

6th grade to 8th grade

9th grade to 12th grade

College

▶ **What milestones have you celebrated with your family?** *(please circle)*

Milestone 1: Birth of a Child

Milestone 2: Faith Commitment

Milestone 3: Preparing for Adolescence

Milestone 4: Commitment to Purity

Milestone 5: Passage to Adulthood

Milestone 6: High School Graduation

▶ **How often do you have intentional Faith Talks with your family?** *(please circle)*

Once a day

Once a week

Once a month

Once a year

Never

▶ **Can you identify a specific God Sighting you've shared with your child in the last month?** *(please circle)*

Yes or No

CHART
YOUR COURSE
Checklist

In Order of Importance

☐ Determine the date of the next one-day Parent Summit. They are offered twice a year. Register online.

☐ Take the two Core Courses offered at every Parent Summit:
1) Understanding and Practicing Legacy Milestones
2) How to Lead a Faith Talk

☐ Core Courses are offered at every Parent Summit or once a semester on Wednesday evenings.

☐ Determine what milestones your children are heading toward in their spiritual development.

☐ At the next Parent Summit, take the seminars associated with the milestones your children are growing toward. Take Parent Seminars 1-2 years before your child is ready to celebrate a milestone.

☐ Purchase resources, available at the Legacy Resource Center on Kingsland's campus, recommended for the milestone your child is working toward.

☐ Set aside time each week for your intentional Faith Talk.

☐ Use recommended resources to quickly create Faith Talks that will lead your family along the pathway.

☐ Celebrate milestones when they are reached, as recommended in the parent seminars. Feel free to be creative and add your own family twist to the celebrations. Then move forward toward the next milestones.

Child's Name	Milestone Celebrated	Upcoming Milestone
_____	_____	_____
_____	_____	_____
_____	_____	_____
_____	_____	_____

Milestone 1
The Birth of a Baby

Milestone 2
Faith
Commitment

Milestone 3
Preparing
for Adolescence

Milestone 4
Commitment
to Purity

Milestone 5
Passage to
Adulthood

Milestone 6
High School
Graduation

Milestone 7
Life in Christ

Resource List

Here's a starter list of resources, organized by milestones, from our Legacy Resource Center. Complete, up-to-date resource lists can be found online at legacymilestones.com and at group.com. Check in often because resources change over time.

Milestone 1

Bedtime Blessings Vol. 2: 100 Bedtime Stories and Activities for Blessing Your Child by John T. Trent (Focus)

Complete Marriage and Family Home Reference Guide by Dr. James Dobson (Tyndale House Publishers)

God and Me!: Devotions for Girls: Ages 2-5 by Lynn Marie-Ittner Klammer (Legacy Press)

Gotta Have God: Fun Devotions for Boys: Ages 2-5 by Lynn Marie-Ittner Klammer (Legacy Press)

Spiritual Growth of Children by Kurt Bruner, John Trent, and Rick Osborne (Focus)

Milestone 2

The Five Love Languages of Children by Gary Chapman and Ross Campbell (Northfield)

Foundation Verse (Children Desiring God)

Gotta Have God : Cool Devotions for Boys: Ages 6-9 by Diane Cory (Legacy Press)

Parent Link: Online monthly newsletter for families; theparentlink.com (Group)

The Story of Me by Stan Jones, Brenda Jones, and Joel Spector (NavPress)

Your Boy: Raising a Godly Son in an Ungodly World by Vicki Courtney (B&H Group)

Your Girl: Raising a Godly Daughter in an Ungodly World by Vicki Courtney (B&H Group)

Milestone 3

God and Me!: Devotions for Girls: Ages 10-12 by Linda Washington (Legacy Press)

Gotta Have God: Cool Devotions for Boys: Ages 10-12 by Linda Washington and Jeanette Dall

(Legacy Press)

How and When to Tell Your Kids about Sex: A Lifelong Approach to Shaping Your Child's Sexual Character by Brenna Jones and Stan Jones (NavPress)

Logged On and Tuned Out: A Non-Techie's Guide to Parenting a Tech-Savvy Generation by Vicki Courtney (B&H Books)

Preparing for Adolescence (Family CD Repack): How to Survive the Coming Years of Change by James C. Dobson (Regal)

Milestone 4

30 Days: Turning the Hearts of Parents & Teenagers Toward Each Other by Richard Ross and Gus Reyes (LifeWay Christian Resources)

Every Young Man's Battle: Strategies for Victory in the Real World of Sexual Temptation by Stephen Arterburn, Fred Stoeker, and Mike Yorkey (Waterbrook Press)

Every Young Woman's Battle: Guarding Your Mind, Heart, and Body in a Sex-Saturated World by Shannon Ethridge and Stephen Arterburn (Crown)

Five Conversations You Must Have with Your Daughter by Vicki Courtney (B&H Books)

Questions You Can't Ask Your Mama about Sex by Craig Gross and Mike Foster (Zondervan)

Milestone 5

The Five Love Languages of Teenagers by Gary Chapman (Northfield)

Raising a Modern-Day Knight: A Father's Role in Guiding His Son to Authentic Manhood by Robert Lewis (Tyndale House)

Parent's Guide to the Spiritual Mentoring of Teens by Joe White and Jim Weidmann (Focus)

Milestone 6

The Blessing by Gary Smalley and John Trent (Thomas Nelson)

The Ever-Loving Truth: Can Faith Thrive in a Post-Christian Culture? by Voddie Baucham (B&H Group)

How to Stay Christian in College by J. Budziszewski (NavPress)

Opie Doesn't Live Here Anymore: Where Faith, Family, and Culture Collide by Walt Mueller (Standard)

Milestone 7

Dangerous Surrender: What Happens When You Say Yes to God by Kay Warren (Zondervan)

Extreme Grandparenting: The Ride of Your Life! by Tim Kimmel and Darcy Kimmel (Focus)

The Jesus Creed: Loving God, Loving Others by Scot McKnight (Paraclete Press)

Prayer: Does It Make Any Difference? by Philip Yancey (Zondervan)

Revolutionary Parenting: What the Research Shows Really Works by George Barna (Barna Books)

Velvet Elvis: Repainting the Christian Faith by Rob Bell (Zondervan)

Wild Goose Chase by Mark Batterson (Multnomah)

About the Author

Brian Haynes serves as associate pastor overseeing spiritual formation at Kingsland Baptist Church in Katy, Texas. Brian is the creator of the Legacy Milestones strategy, designed to inseparably link church and home to equip the generations.

He's married to his high school sweetheart, Angela, and they have three daughters, Hailey, Madelyn, and Eden. Brian is a graduate of Baylor University, Southwestern Seminary, and Liberty Theological Seminary, where he earned a Doctor of Ministry for his work in discipleship and family ministry.

Brian's passion in ministry is to build a strategic bridge between the Shema and the Great Commission, helping families and churches effectively disciple the generations.

For more information on Brian Haynes and to join an ongoing conversation about developing legacy at home and church, visit these websites:

legacymilestones.com

kingsland.org

legacyblog.org

Check out these other family ministry resources at Group.com...

FaithWeaver™: Integrated Sunday school curriculum for families— from preschool level through senior adulthood

The Family-Friendly Church by Ben Freudenburg with Rick Lawrence

Grand Days: Ideas for Sharing Faith Moments Between Grandparents and Grandkids

Parent Link: Online, customizable monthly newsletter for families

Passing the Baton: Guide Your Child to Follow Jesus